THE COKESBURY MARRIAGE
MANUAL

THE COKESBURY
MARRIAGE MANUAL

Edited by

WILLIAM H. LEACH

Revised and Enlarged Edition

ABINGDON PRESS
Nashville • New York

THE COKESBURY MARRIAGE MANUAL

ISBN 0-687-08788-0

Library of Congress Catalog Card Number: 59-10364

SET UP, PRINTED, AND BOUND BY THE
PARTHENON PRESS, AT NASHVILLE,
TENNESSEE, UNITED STATES OF AMERICA

PREFACE TO THE REVISED
AND ENLARGED EDITION

The first edition of this book was issued by the Cokesbury Press in 1933. The first revised edition bears the date of 1939. A third edition was dated 1945. This then is the third revised edition.

Each revised edition has been more than a reprinting. Social ideas change regarding marriage, and even the church pronouncements differ from those of a generation ago. Changes in the state laws have not been too great, but it has been felt wise to insert in the pages the results of the latest legislation.

WILLIAM H. LEACH

CONTENTS

THE PROTESTANT EPISCOPAL
SERVICE

From *The Book of Common Prayer*

At the day and time appointed for Solemnization of Matrimony, the Persons to be married shall come into the body of the Church, or shall be ready in some proper house, with their friends and neighbours; and there standing together, the Man on the right hand, and the Woman on the left, the Minister shall say,

Dearly beloved, we are gathered together here in the sight of God, and in the face of this company, to join together this Man and this Woman in holy Matrimony; which is an honourable estate, instituted of God, signifying unto us the mystical union that is betwixt Christ and his Church: which holy estate Christ adorned and beautified with his presence and first miracle that he wrought in Cana of Galilee, and is commended of Saint Paul to be honourable among all men: and therefore is not by any to be entered into unadvisedly or lightly; but reverently, discreetly, advisedly, soberly, and in the fear of God. Into this holy estate these two persons present come now to be joined. If any man can show just cause, why they may not lawfully be joined together, let him now speak, or else hereafter for ever hold his peace.

And also speaking unto the Persons who are to be married, he shall say,

I REQUIRE and charge you both, as ye will answer at the dreadful day of judgment when the secrets of all hearts shall be disclosed, that if either of you know any impediment, why ye may not be lawfully joined together in Matrimony, ye do now confess it. For be ye well assured, that if any persons are joined together otherwise than as God's Word doth allow, their marriage is not lawful.

The Minister, if he shall have reason to doubt of the lawfulness of the proposed Marriage, may demand sufficient surety for his indemnification: but if no impediment shall be alleged, or suspected, the Minister shall say to the Man,

N. WILT thou have this Woman to thy wedded wife, to live together after God's ordinance in the holy estate of Matrimony? Wilt thou love her, comfort her, honour, and keep her in sickness and in health; and, forsaking all others, keep thee only unto her, so long as ye both shall live?

The Man shall answer,

I will.

Then shall the Minister say unto the Woman,

N. WILT thou have this Man to thy wedded husband, to live together after God's ordinance in the holy estate of Matrimony? Wilt thou love him, comfort him, honour, and keep him in sickness and in health; and, forsaking all others, keep thee only unto him, so long as ye both shall live?

The Woman shall answer,

I will.

Then shall the Minister say,

Who giveth this Woman to be married to this Man?

Then shall they give their troth to each other in this manner. The Minister, receiving the Woman at her father's or friend's hand, shall cause the Man with his right hand to take the Woman by her right hand, and to say after him as followeth.

I *N*. take thee *N*. to my wedded Wife, to have and to hold from this day forward, for better for worse, for richer for poorer, in sickness and in health, to love and to cherish, till death us do part, according to God's holy ordinance; and thereto I plight thee my troth.

Then shall they loose their hands; and the Woman with her right hand taking the Man by his right hand, shall likewise say after the Minister,

I *N*. take thee *N*. to my wedded Husband, to have and to hold from this day forward, for better for worse, for richer for poorer, in sickness and in health, to love and to cherish, till death us do part, according to God's holy ordinance; and thereto I give thee my troth.

Then shall they again loose their hands; and the Man shall give unto the Woman a Ring on this wise: the Minister taking the Ring shall deliver it unto the Man, to put it upon the fourth finger of the Woman's left hand. And the Man holding the Ring there, and taught by the Minister, shall say,

WITH this Ring I thee wed: In the Name of the Father, and of the Son, and of the Holy Ghost. Amen.

And, before delivering the Ring to the Man, the Minister may say as followeth.

BLESS, O Lord, this Ring, that he who gives it and she who wears it may abide in thy peace, and continue in thy favour, unto their life's end; through Jesus Christ our Lord. Amen.

Then, the Man leaving the Ring upon the fourth finger of the Woman's left hand, the Minister shall say,

Let us pray.

Then shall the Minister and the People, still standing, say the Lord's Prayer.

OUR Father, who art in heaven, Hallowed be thy Name. Thy kingdom come. Thy will be done, On earth as it is in heaven. Give us this day our daily bread. And forgive us our trespasses, As we forgive those who trespass against us. And lead us not into temptation, But deliver us from evil. For thine is the kingdom, and the power, and the glory, for ever and ever. Amen.

Then shall the Minister add,

O ETERNAL God, Creator and Preserver of all mankind, Giver of all spiritual grace, the Author of everlasting life; Send thy blessing upon these thy servants, this man and this woman, whom we bless in thy Name; that they, living faithfully together, may surely perform and keep the vow and covenant betwixt them made, (whereof this Ring given and received is a token and pledge,) and may ever remain in perfect love and peace together, and live according to thy laws; through Jesus Christ our Lord. *Amen.*

The Minister may add one or both of the following prayers.

O ALMIGHTY God, Creator of mankind, who only art the well-spring of life; Bestow upon these thy servants, if it be thy will, the gift and heritage of children; and grant that they may see their children brought up in thy faith and fear, to the honour and glory of thy Name; through Jesus Christ our Lord. *Amen.*

O GOD, who hast so consecrated the state of Matrimony that in it is represented the spiritual marriage and unity betwixt Christ and his Church; Look mercifully upon these thy servants, that they may love, honour, and cherish each other, and so live together in faithfulness and patience, in wisdom and true

godliness, that their home may be a haven of
blessing and of peace; through the same Jesus
Christ our Lord, who liveth and reigneth with
thee and the Holy Spirit ever, one God, world
without end. *Amen.*

*Then shall the Minister join their right hands to-
gether, and say,*

Those whom God hath joined together let
no man put asunder.

Then shall the Minister speak unto the company.

FORASMUCH as *N.* and *N.* have consented
together in holy wedlock, and have witnessed the same before God and this company,
and thereto have given and pledged their
troth, each to the other, and have declared
the same by giving and receiving a Ring, and
by joining hands; I pronounce that they are
Man and Wife, In the Name of the Father,
and of the Son, and of the Holy Ghost. Amen.

*The Man and Wife kneeling, the Minister shall add
this Blessing.*

GOD the Father, God the Son, God the
Holy Ghost, bless, preserve, and keep
you; the Lord mercifully with his favour look
upon you, and fill you with all spiritual bene-

diction and grace; that ye may so live together in this life, that in the world to come ye may have life everlasting. *Amen.*

The laws respecting Matrimony, whether by publishing the Banns in Churches, or by Licence, being different in the several States, every minister is left to the direction of those laws, in every thing that regards the civil contract between the parties.

And when the Banns are published, it shall be in the following form:

I PUBLISH the Banns of Marriage between N. of —, and N. of —. If any of you know cause, or just impediment, why these two persons should not be joined together in holy Matrimony, ye are to declare it. This is the first [second *or* third] time of asking.

A LUTHERAN SERVICE

From the *Common Service Book* [1]

*Before solemnizing a Marriage, the Minister shall
diligently inquire: First, as to whether the union
contemplated be in accordance with the Word of
God; Second, whether it be in accordance with
the Laws of the State. No Marriage shall be
solemnized unless the Minister be convinced that
God's blessing may properly be asked upon it.*

*The Minister may publish the Banns in the church,
one or more Sundays before the day appointed
for the Marriage, saying:*

N. N. AND N. N. purpose to enter into the
holy estate of Matrimony, according to God's
ordinance. They desire that prayer be made
for them, that they may enter into this union
in the Name of the Lord, and be prospered in
it. If any one can show just cause why they
may not be joined together, I exhort him to
make known such objection before the day of
marriage.

When a Marriage is solemnized in the Church, a

[1] Copyright by the United Lutheran Church in America.

17

Hymn may be sung, and Psalm 67 or Psalm 128 may be sung or said, ending with the Gloria Patri.

When a Marriage is solemnized in the home, the rubrics pertaining to the Chancel and the Altar shall be disregarded.

The Persons to be married having presented themselves at the entrance to the Chancel, the Man to the right of the Woman, the Minister shall say:

IN the Name of the Father, and of the Son, and of the Holy Ghost. *Amen.*

Dearly Beloved: Forasmuch as Marriage is a holy estate, ordained of God, and to be held in honor by all, it becometh those who enter therein to weigh, with reverent minds, what the Word of God teacheth concerning it:

The Lord God said, It is not good that the man should be alone; I will make him an helpmeet for him.

Our Lord Jesus Christ said: Have ye not read that He which made them at the beginning, made them male and female, and said, For this cause shall a man leave father and mother, and shall cleave to his wife; and they twain shall be one flesh? Wherefore, they are no more twain, but one flesh. What therefore

God hath joined together, let not man put asunder.

The Apostle Paul, speaking by the Holy Spirit, saith: Husbands, love your wives, even as Christ also loved the Church, and gave Himself for it. Wives, submit yourselves unto your own husbands, as unto the Lord.

And although, by reason of sin, many a cross hath been laid thereon, nevertheless our gracious Father in heaven doth not forsake his children in an estate so holy and acceptable to Him, but is ever present with His abundant blessing.

Into this holy estate, this Man and this Woman come now to be united. If any one, therefore, can show just cause why they may not be lawfully joined together, let him now speak, or else forever hold his peace.

Then shall the Minister say to the Man:

N., wilt thou have this Woman to thy wedded wife, to live together after God's ordinance in the holy estate of Matrimony? Wilt thou love her, comfort her, honor and keep her in sickness and in health, and, forsaking all others, keep thee only unto her, so long as ye both shall live?

The Man shall say:

I will.

Then shall the Minister say to the Woman:

N., WILT thou have this Man to thy wedded husband, to live together after
God's ordinance in the holy estate of Matrimony? Wilt thou love him, comfort him,
honor and keep him in sickness and in health,
and, forsaking all others, keep thee only unto
him, so long as ye both shall live?

The Woman shall say:

I will.

*If the Woman be Given in Marriage, the Minister
shall now receive her at the hands of her father
(or guardian or any friend), the Woman placing
her right hand in the hand of the Minister. Then
shall the Minister place the right hand of the
Woman in the right hand of the Man. Then shall
they loose their hands.*

*Then shall the Minister precede the Man and the
Woman to the Altar. The Man shall take the
right hand of the Woman and say after the Minister:*

I, N., take thee, N., to my wedded Wife,
and plight thee my troth, till death us do
part.

*Then shall the Woman, in like manner, say after
    the Minister:*

I, N., take thee, N., to my wedded Husband, and plight thee my troth, till death
us do part.

*If the wedding Ring be used, the Minister shall now
    receive it and give it to the Man to put on the
    fourth finger of the Woman's left hand. Then
    shall the Man say, or if two rings be used, the
    Man and the Woman, in turn, shall say, after
    the Minister:*

Receive this Ring as a token of wedded love
and troth.

Then shall the Minister say:

Join your right hands.

*Then shall the Minister lay his right hand upon their
    hands and say:*

FORASMUCH as N. and N. have consented together in holy wedlock, and have declared
the same before God and in the presence of
this company, I pronounce them Man and
Wife, In the Name of the Father, and of the
Son, and of the Holy Ghost. Amen.

What God hath joined together, let not
man put asunder.

*Then may they kneel and the Minister may bless
them, saying:*

THE Lord God, Who created our first parents and sanctified their union in Marriage: Sanctify and bless you, that ye may
please Him both in body and soul, and live
together in holy love until life's end. Amen.

Then shall the Minister say:

Let us pray.

ALMIGHTY and most Merciful God, Who
hast now united this man and this woman
in the holy estate of Matrimony: Grant them
grace to live therein according to Thy Holy
Word; strengthen them in constant fidelity
and true affection toward each other; sustain
and defend them amidst all trials and temptations; and help them so to pass through this
world in faith toward Thee, in communion
with Thy Holy Church, and in loving service
one of the other, that they may enjoy forever
Thy heavenly benediction; through Jesus
Christ, Thy Son, our Lord, Who liveth and
reigneth with Thee and the Holy Ghost,
ever One God, world without end. *Amen.*

Then shall all say:

OUR Father, Who art in heaven; Hallowed be Thy Name; Thy kingdom come; Thy will be done on earth, as it is in heaven; Give us this day our daily bread; And forgive us our trespasses, as we forgive those who trespass against us; And lead us not into temptation; But deliver us from evil; For Thine is the kingdom, and the power, and the glory, for ever and ever. Amen.

Then shall the Minister say the Benediction:

THE Lord bless you, and keep you. The Lord make His face shine upon you, and be gracious unto you. The Lord lift up his countenance upon you, and give you peace. *Amen.*

THE METHODIST SERVICE

From *The Ritual* [1]

*At the time appointed, the persons to be married—
having been qualified according to the law of the
state and the standards of the church—standing together facing the minister, the man at the minister's left hand and the woman at the right, the
minister shall say:*

DEARLY beloved, we are gathered here in
the sight of God, and in the presence of
these witnesses, to join together this man and
this woman in holy matrimony; which is an
honorable estate, instituted of God, and signifying unto us the mystical union which
exists between Christ and his Church; which
holy estate Christ adorned and beautified with
his presence in Cana of Galilee. It is therefore
not to be entered into unadvisedly, but reverently, discreetly, and in the fear of God. Into
this holy estate these two persons come now
to be joined.

[1] In *Doctrines and Discipline of The Methodist Church;*
copyright © 1957 by The Board of Publication of The
Methodist Church, Inc.

24

Speaking to the persons to be married, the minister shall say:

I REQUIRE and charge you both, as you stand in the presence of God, to remember that love and loyalty alone will avail as the foundation of a happy and enduring home. No other human ties are more tender, no other vows more sacred than those you now assume. If these solemn vows be kept inviolate, and if steadfastly you endeavor to do the will of your heavenly Father, your life will be full of joy, and the home which you are establishing will abide in peace.

Then shall the minister say to the man, using his Christian name:

N., WILT thou have this woman to be thy wedded wife, to live together in the holy estate of matrimony? Wilt thou love her, comfort her, honor and keep her, in sickness and in health; and forsaking all other keep thee only unto her, so long as ye both shall live?

The man shall answer:

I will.

Then shall the minister say to the woman, using her Christian name:

N., WILT thou have this man to be thy wedded husband, to live together in the holy estate of matrimony? Wilt thou love him, comfort him, honor and keep him, in sickness and in health; and forsaking all other keep thee only unto him, so long as ye both shall live?

The woman shall answer:

I will.

Then may the minister say:

Who giveth this woman to be married to this man?

The father of the woman, or whoever giveth her in marriage, shall answer:

I do.

Then the minister (receiving the hand of the woman from her father or other sponsor) shall cause the man with his right hand to take the woman by her right hand, and say after him:

I N., take thee, N., to be my wedded wife, to have and to hold, from this day forward, for better, for worse, for richer, for poorer, in sickness and in health, to love and to cherish, till death us do part, according to God's holy ordinance; and thereto I plight thee my troth.

Then shall they loose their hands; and the woman, with her right hand taking the man by his right hand, shall say after the minister:

I, *N.*, take thee, *N.*, to be my wedded husband, to have and to hold, from this day forward, for better, for worse, for richer, for poorer, in sickness and in health, to love and to cherish, till death us do part, according to God's holy ordinance; and thereto I plight thee my troth.

Then shall they again loose their hands; and they may give unto each other rings, or the man may give unto the woman a ring, on this wise: the minister, taking the ring or rings, shall say:

THE wedding ring is an outward and visible sign of an inward and spiritual grace, signifying unto all the uniting of this man and this woman in holy matrimony, through the Church of Jesus Christ our Lord.

Then the minister may say:

Let us pray.

Bless, O Lord, the giving of these rings, that they who wear them may abide forever in thy peace, and continue in thy favor; through Jesus Christ our Lord. *Amen.*

Or, if there be but one ring, the minister may say:

Bless, O Lord, the giving of this ring, that he who gives it and she who wears it may abide forever in thy peace, and continue in thy favor, through Jesus Christ our Lord. *Amen.*

The minister shall then deliver the proper ring to the man to put upon the third finger of the woman's left hand. The man, holding the ring there, shall say after the minister:

In token and pledge of the vow between us made, with this ring I thee wed; in the name of the Father, and of the Son, and of the Holy Spirit. Amen.

Then, if there be a second ring, the minister shall deliver it to the woman to put upon the third finger of the man's left hand; and the woman, holding the ring there, shall say after the minister:

In token and pledge of the vow between us made, with this ring I thee wed; in the name of the Father, and of the Son, and of the Holy Spirit. Amen.

Then shall the minister say:

Let us pray.

O ETERNAL God, creator and preserver of all mankind, giver of all spiritual grace, the author of everlasting life; send thy blessing upon this man and this woman, whom we bless in thy name; that they may surely perform and keep the vow and covenant between them made, and may ever remain in perfect love and peace together, and live according to thy laws.

Look graciously upon them, that they may love, honor and cherish each other, and so live together in faithfulness and patience, in wisdom and true godliness, that their home may be a haven of blessing and a place of peace; through Jesus Christ our Lord. Amen.

Then shall the minister join their right hands together and with his hand on their united hands shall say:

FORASMUCH as *N.* and *N.* have consented together in holy wedlock, and have witnessed the same before God and this company, and thereto have pledged their troth each to the other, and have declared the same by joining hands (and by giving and receiving *a ring*); I pronounce that they are husband and wife together, in the name of the Father, and of the Son, and of the Holy Spirit. Those whom God hath joined together, let not man put asunder. *Amen.*

Then, the husband and wife kneeling, the minister shall say:

Let us pray.

OUR Father who art in heaven, hallowed be thy name; thy kingdom come; thy will be done on earth as it is in heaven. Give us this day our daily bread. And forgive us our trespasses, as we forgive those who trespass against us. And lead us not into temptation, but deliver us from evil. For thine is the kingdom, and the power, and the glory, forever. Amen.

Then shall the minister add this blessing:

GOD the Father, the Son, and the Holy Spirit, bless, preserve, and keep you; the Lord graciously with his favor look upon you, and so fill you with all spiritual benediction and love that you may so live together in this life that in the world to come you may have life everlasting. *Amen.*

THE PRESBYTERIAN SERVICE

From *The Book of Common Worship* [1]

Forasmuch as marriage is a sacred relation, the ground of human fellowship and society, and most precious to mankind; although it be not a Sacrament nor peculiar to the Church of Christ, it is proper that it be solemnized by a lawful minister, that he may give counsel from the Word of God to those entering holy wedlock, and invoke the divine blessing upon them.—Directory for Worship, Chap. XII.

The persons to be married shall present themselves before the Minister, the Woman standing at the left hand of the Man. Then, all present reverently standing, the Minister shall say to the company:

D EARLY beloved, we are assembled here in the presence of God, to join this Man and this Woman in holy Marriage; which is instituted of God, regulated by His commandments, blessed by our Lord Jesus Christ, and to be held in honor among all men. Let

[1] Revised edition; copyright, 1932, by the Board of Christian Education of the Presbyterian Church in the U. S. A.

us therefore reverently remember that God has established and sanctified Marriage, for the welfare and happiness of mankind. Our Saviour has declared that a man shall forsake his father and mother and cleave unto his wife. By His apostles, He has instructed those who enter into this relation to cherish a mutual esteem and love; to bear with each other's infirmities and weaknesses; to comfort each other in sickness, trouble, and sorrow; in honesty and industry to provide for each other and for their household in temporal things; to pray for and encourage each other in the things which pertain to God; and to live together as heirs of the grace of life.

Then, speaking unto the persons who are to be married, he shall say:

FORASMUCH as you have come hither to be made one in this blessed estate, I charge you both, that if either of you know any reason why you may not rightly be joined together in Marriage, you do now acknowledge it. For be well assured that if any persons are joined together otherwise than as God's Word allows, their union is not blessed by Him.

Then, if no obstacle appears, the Minister shall say:

Let us pray.

ALMIGHTY and ever blessed God, whose presence is the happiness of every condition, and whose favor sweetens every relation; we beseech Thee to be present and favorable unto these Thy servants, that they may be truly joined in the honorable estate of Marriage. As Thou hast brought them together by Thy providence, sanctify them by Thy Spirit, giving them a new frame of heart for their new estate; and grant unto them, now in the hour of their affiance and throughout their wedded life, Thy heavenly guidance; through our Lord Jesus Christ. *Amen.*

Then the Minister shall say to the Man:

M——, wilt thou have this Woman to be thy wife, and wilt thou pledge thy troth to her, in all love and honor, in all duty and service, in all faith and tenderness, to live with her and cherish her, according to the ordinance of God, in the holy bond of Marriage?

The Man shall answer:

I will.

Then the Minister shall say to the Woman:

N——, wilt thou have this Man to be thy husband, and wilt thou pledge thy troth to him, in all love and honor, in all duty and service, in all faith and tenderness, to live with him and cherish him, according to the ordinance of God, in the holy bond of Marriage?

The Woman shall answer:

I will.

Then the Minister may say:

Who giveth this Woman to be married to this Man?

Then the father (or guardian or any friend) of the Woman shall put her right hand into the hand of the Minister, who shall cause the Man with his right hand to take the Woman by her right hand and to say after him as follows:

I, M., take thee N., To be my wedded wife; and I do promise and covenant; Before God and these witnesses; To be thy loving and faithful husband; In plenty and in want; In joy and in sorrow; In sickness and in health; As long as we both shall live.

*Then shall they loose their hands; and the Woman
with her right hand taking the Man by his right
hand, shall likewise say after the Minister:*

I, *N.*, take thee *M.*; To be my wedded husband; And I do promise and covenant;
Before God and these witnesses; To be thy
loving and faithful wife; In plenty and in
want; In joy and in sorrow; In sickness and
in health; As long as we both shall live.

*Then, if a ring be provided it shall be given by the
Man to the Woman, and by the Woman to the
Minister, who shall then return it to the Man,
who shall put it upon the fourth finger of the
Woman's left hand, saying after the Minister:*

This Ring I give thee, In token and pledge,
Of our constant faith, And abiding love.

Then the Minister shall say:

Let us pray.

Most merciful and gracious God, of whom
the whole family in heaven and earth is
named; bestow upon these Thy servants the
seal of Thine approval, and Thy fatherly
benediction; granting unto them grace to ful-
fil, with pure and steadfast affection, the vow
and covenant between them made. Guide

them together, we beseech Thee, in the happy way of righteousness and peace, that loving and serving Thee, with one heart and mind, all the days of their life, they may be abundantly enriched with the tokens of Thine everlasting grace, in Jesus Christ our Lord. *Amen.*

OUR Father, who art in heaven, Hallowed be Thy Name. Thy kingdom come. Thy will be done, On earth as it is in heaven. Give us this day our daily bread. And forgive us our debts, As we forgive our debtors. And lead us not into temptation, But deliver us from evil: For thine is the kingdom, and the power, and the glory, for ever. *Amen.*

Then shall the Minister say unto all who are present:

BY the authority committed unto me as a Minister of the Church of Christ, I declare that *M.* and *N.* are now Husband and Wife, according to the ordinance of God, and the law of this State: in the Name of the Father, and of the Son, and of the Holy Spirit. *Amen.*

Then, causing the Husband and Wife to join their right hands, the Minister shall say:

Whom God hath joined together, let no man put asunder.

And the Minister shall pronounce this BLESSING:

THE Lord bless you and keep you: The Lord make his face shine upon you and be gracious unto you:

The Lord lift up his countenance upon you and give you peace:

Both now and in the life everlasting. *Amen.*

TWO BAPTIST SERVICES [1]

I

Minister

D EARLY beloved, we are gathered together here in the sight of God, and in the presence of this company, to join together this man and this woman in holy matrimony.

Marriage is an honorable estate, instituted of God, blessed by our Lord Jesus Christ, and commended by St. Paul to be honorable among all men.

It is not, therefore, to be entered into lightly or unadvisedly; but reverently, soberly, and in the fear of God.

It is fitting, therefore, that we should, on this occasion, seek the divine blessing. Let us pray.

[1] The Baptist churches are strictly nonliturgical, and no special service is authorized. The following services were compiled by Warren E. Jackson, a Baptist clergyman of The American Baptist Convention and Louie D. Newton of the Southern Baptist Convention.

(An informal prayer follows.)

To the Man

M., DO you take this woman to be your lawful wedded wife? And do you solemnly promise, before God and these witnesses, that you will love, honor, and cherish her; and that, forsaking all others for her alone, you will perform unto her all the duties that a husband owes to his wife, until God, by death, shall separate you?

The Man

I do.

To the Woman

N., DO you take this man to be your lawful wedded husband? And do you solemnly promise, before God and these witnesses, that you will love, honor, and cherish him; and that, forsaking all others for him alone, you will perform unto him all the duties that a wife owes to her husband, until God, by death, shall separate you?

The Woman

I do.

WHEN THE WOMAN IS GIVEN AWAY

To the Giver

Who giveth this woman to be married to this man?

The Giver

I do.

(*Places woman's hand in hand of minister. Retires to seat.*)

To the Two

Since it is your desire to take each other as husband and wife, you will please indicate this desire by joining your right hands, and by repeating in this presence the marriage vow.

The Man

I, *M.*, take thee *N.*, to be my wedded wife, to have and to hold, from this day forward, for better or for worse, for richer or for poorer, in sickness and in health, to love and to cherish, till death do us part, according to God's holy ordinance, and thereto I pledge thee my faith.

The Woman

I N., take thee, M., to be my wedded husband, to have and to hold, from this day forward, for better or for worse, for richer or for poorer, in sickness and in health, to love and to cherish, till death do us part, according to God's holy ordinance, and thereto I pledge thee my faith.

FOR THE RING SERVICE

To the Man

WHAT token do you give as a symbol of your affection and of your sincerity and fidelity?

The Man

A ring.

(*Takes ring from best man and gives it to minister.*)

To the Woman

WILL you receive this ring as a token of M.'s affection, sincerity, and fidelity, and will you wear it as a symbol of your own affection, sincerity, and fidelity toward him?

The Woman

I will.

To the Man

You will place the ring on *N.'s* left hand and repeat the vow of the ring.

The Man

THIS ring I give thee, in token and pledge of our constant faith and abiding love; with this ring I thee wed, and with all my earthly goods I thee endow.

To the Company

FORASMUCH as *M.* and *N.* have consented together in holy wedlock, and have witnessed the same before God and this company, and have thereto given and pledged their faith, each to the other, and have declared the same by joining their right hands, I pronounce that they are husband and wife, in the name of the Father, and of the Son, and of the Holy Spirit.

Those whom God hath joined together, let not man put asunder!

Let us pray.

O ETERNAL God, Creator and Preserver of all mankind, Giver of all spiritual grace, and Author of everlasting life; send thy blessing upon these thy servants, this man and this woman, whom we bless in thy name; that they may surely keep and perform the vow and covenant between them made, and that they may ever remain in perfect love and peace together, and may live according to thy laws; through Jesus Christ our Lord.

And now may the God of all righteousness bless, preserve, and keep you; may the Lord mercifully with his favor look upon you, and fill you with all spiritual benediction and grace; that ye may so live together in this life that in the world to come you may have everlasting life in the presence of God; through our Lord Jesus Christ. *Amen*.

II

Who gives this woman in marriage?

Father will answer:

I do.

Minister

We are gathered, my friends, to witness rites belonging to an institution as old as the human race. Marriage was founded by our Father in the Garden of Eden and there witnessed by the angels. Marriage, then, is divine —divine in its origin, and its vows should never be lightly assumed. Hence, how grateful we are when friends come as you have, that you may have not only the sanction of the state, but the blessing of religion as well.

And now if you wish me to proceed with the ceremony, you will please join your right hands.

To the Man

Do you, _____, take this woman whom you hold by the right hand to be your true and lawful wife? And do you promise to cleave unto her, and her alone, as long as life shall last?

Man answers:

I do.

To the Woman

Do you, ――, take this man whom you hold by the right hand to be your true and lawful husband? And do you promise to cleave unto him, and him alone, as long as life shall last?

Woman answers:

I do.

To the Man

And now do you wish to use the rings in taking these vows?

Man answers:

We do.

Rings are handed to minister, who says:

These rings, being circles, are symbolic of eternity and, being made of precious metal, are symbolic of the pure love which has already united your hearts.

The groom will please take the ring, which he presents to the bride, and placing it on her finger, repeat after me: "With this ring I thee wed, and with all my heart's affection I thee endow."

(Same words for the bride as she places ring on the groom's finger.)

And now, will you please repeat after me a beautiful troth:

> Entreat me not to leave thee,
> Or to return from following after thee:
> For whither thou goest, I will go;
> And where thou lodgest, I will lodge:
> Thy people shall be my people,
> And thy God my God.

And now, by the authority vested in me as a minister of the gospel by the commonwealth of Georgia, and in the name of the Father and of the Son and of the Holy Spirit, I pronounce you man and wife. Therefore, what God hath joined together, let not man put asunder.

Let us pray: Our Father, we thank thee for this sacred and beautiful institution which we call marriage, given of thee and blessed by thee through all the ages. We thank thee for these friends who have come to profess publicly their love, and to announce their purpose to build their home. Grant that they may have long life, and good health, and true prosperity. And bless these their friends. In the name of him who gave his blessing to a wedding scene in Cana, even Jesus Christ our Lord. *Amen.*

AN IAN MACLAREN SERVICE [1]

Dear Friends of Us All: Your love is to be crowned with the Blessings of the Church, which is the bride of Christ, and your feet are soon to stand within the goodly Land of Promise.

You are entering into that holy estate which is the deepest mystery of experience and the very sacrament of Divine Love.

It is a chief moment in life when two people, who were strangers to one another, are drawn together by an irresistible attraction, so that their souls cannot be henceforth divided by time or space; when one sees in a single woman that dream of purity and sweetness which has ever haunted his soul; when in a single man she finds the rest and satisfaction her heart has been unconsciously seeking. It is a revelation from above, and makes all things new; it is the hand of Provi-

[1] Arranged by Carl H. Elliott. The distinctive feature of it is the opening address, which is taken from *Kate Carnegie* (English edition), by Ian Maclaren.

48

dence, and annuls every argument of worldly providence.

You are performing an act of utter faith, believing in one another to the end.

As the bride gives herself to the bridegroom, let him be to her now father and mother, sister and brother, and most sacred—husband. As he gives himself to her, let the bride sustain and inspire his heart in the great affairs of life and in his chosen calling.

If you wish your new estate to be touched with perennial beauty, cherish those gracious visions which have made spring within your hearts during the days of your betrothal. You must never forget nor deny the vision you once saw; you must resolve that it be not blotted out nor blurred by the commonplace experiences of life. Faults may appear which were once hidden in a golden mist; excellencies may seem to fade in the glare of the noonday sun. Still be unmoved in your devotion; still remain confident and hopeful. Amid the reality of present imperfection, believe in the ideal. You saw it once. It still exists. It is the final truth.

This is the man, that is the woman you love. That is the shape of spiritual beauty God sees and which for an hour he showed to you. That is the soul which is to be when this conflict with temptations, hindrances, failures is accomplished. Hide that imagination in your inmost heart. Make real this ideal in your united lives and your home will be a "place of repair and harbor," a dwelling place of contentment and abiding joy, a foretaste of that heavenly habitation where goodness reigns and love is the very air, the kingdom and home of our Father above.

Let us unite in prayer.

OUR Father who art in heaven. At every turning of life's way, we would stop to seek Thy guidance and to plead Thy blessing. We thank Thee that Thou art Love and that Thou hast created us after Thy image.

We thank Thee for planting love for woman in the heart of man, and love for man in the heart of woman. We thank Thee, too, for the noble self-denials and heroic sacrifices that have had this love as their motive, and for all the gladness that has radiated from homes founded upon this rock of inspiring hope, faith, and courage in other lives.

Be here, Lord Jesus, even as Thou wert at

Cana of Galilee, to grace and bless our Wedding Feast. Especially wilt Thou richly bless these two lives now to be made one by this bond of love. May they live each for the other and both for God. May their home be Thy abiding place and Thou their constant guest.

Remember in much mercy and kindness each of us gathered here and all our dear ones far and near. Watch over the homes of our fair land, and may all the families of earth be blessed. In Jesus' name. Amen.

Minister to Bride's Father

D o you, ———, give this woman to wed this man?

Answer

I do.

Minister to Groom

D o you, ———, take ——— before God and these witnesses to be your lawful wedded wife? Do you promise to love and cherish her in joy and sorrow, in health and sickness, in prosperity and adversity, so long as you both shall live?

Answer

I do.

Minister to Bride

Do you, _____, take _____ before God and these witnesses to be your lawful wedded husband? Do you promise to love and honor him in joy and sorrow, in sickness and health, in adversity and prosperity, so long as you both shall live?

Answer

I do.

Minister to Groom

What token do you bring as a pledge that you will faithfully perform these vows?

(Accepts Ring from Groom)

Minister to Both

Let this ring be the sacred symbol of your unchanging love.

(Returns Ring to Groom)

Groom, placing Ring on the finger of Bride

This ring I give you, _____, as a pledge of my abiding loyalty and love.

Bride

I ACCEPT this ring from you, _____, and thus pledge my abiding loyalty and love.

Minister

BY authority of the state given to me as a minister of the Church of Jesus Christ, I now pronounce you husband and wife. Husband, love your wife. Wife, love your husband.

Benediction

THE Lord bless you, and keep you; the Lord make his face shine upon you, and be gracious unto you; the Lord lift up his countenance upon you, and give you peace. *Amen.*

A COMMUNITY CHURCH SERVICE [1]

DEARLY beloved, you are come together in this holy place and in the presence of these witnesses to be united in holy marriage. This is indeed an honorable estate which you seek. Instituted by God in the Garden when he saw that it was not good that man should be alone, marriage was finally given a crown of glory by the Apostle Paul, who likens it unto that holy union which exists between Christ and his Church, in which Christ is called the Bridegroom, and his Church the Bride. Surely it is a blessed union, and it is a holy one in so far as the promises are kept.

You are about to assume mutual relationships and responsibilities. You are about to pledge to each other your undying devotion and fidelity. If there is any reason why you should not do so, I charge you and any of the assembled now to make it known.

Henceforth you will no longer be twain,

[1] Arranged by Frank Nelson, formerly Business Administrator, First Methodist Church, Santa Monica, California.

but of one flesh. Your paths will be parallel, your responsibilities will increase, but your joy will be multiplied if you are sincere and earnest in your relations one with another and with God, with whom you make this covenant.

By coming into this temple of God you hereby recognize that this covenant is not only a legal contract but a bond of union made in heaven, and is therefore to be entered into reverently and discreetly, knowing that God in his heaven will richly bless those who seek his favor. Therefore let us look to him in prayer, knowing that "he is faithful who hath promised."

Let us pray.

All will kneel.

O LORD Jesus, who blessed with thy presence the wedding feast at Cana in Galilee; bless also these thy children who seek thy favor. Look down upon them as their loves are about to be joined. O God, we would never have known love were it not for thee. Thou didst establish it. Thou didst endow us with its tender grace. By thy powerful love, we pray that thou wilt weld these two hearts together and seal them with the bow of promise so that no storm of life, no temptation of the flesh, will be able to shake their faith in one another or in thee. Be with them in sunshine or in shadow, in joy or sorrow, in prosperity or adversity; and may they so live that they may be able to enjoy life everlasting; through Jesus Christ our Lord. *Amen.*

Minister to groom

Wilt thou, _____, take _____ to be thy wedded wife, to live together after God's ordinance in the holy estate of matrimony? Wilt thou love, honor, trust, and serve her in sickness and in health, be true and loyal to her, as long as ye both shall live?

Answer

I will.

Minister to bride

Wilt thou, _____, take _____ to be thy wedded husband, to live together after God's ordinance in the holy estate of matrimony? Wilt thou love, honor, trust, and serve him in sickness and in health, be true and loyal to him, as long as ye both shall live?

Answer

I will.

Minister to groom

WHAT token do you give in commemoration of this pledge?

The groom hands the ring to the bride, who hands it to the minister. The minister, in turn, hands it back to the groom, who places it on the fourth finger of the bride's left hand. He continues to hold the ring in position.

To groom

DOST thou, _____, give this ring in pledge that thou wilt keep this promise and perform these vows?

Answer

I do.

To bride

DOST thou, _____, receive this ring in pledge that thou wilt keep this promise and perform these vows?

Answer

I do.

Groom

WITH this token of fidelity, before this holy altar, in the presence of God Almighty, I thee wed.

The bride and groom now join their right hands.

Minister

FORASMUCH, then, as you, _____, and you, _____, have consented together in holy wedlock, and have pledged your undying devotion to each other, I therefore, ministering in God's name and by authority of the state, pronounce you husband and wife.

What, therefore, God hath joined together, let not man put asunder.

Henceforth you go down life's pathway together. Let love be the charmed word in the dialect of your home and hearts. May the circle of the ring typify your unending happiness, and may the triangle formed in its passing, one to another, and then to me, ministering in God's name, signify that triune relationship with him who reigns above where marriages are made. May Christ be the head of your house. May he be the unseen guest at every meal, the silent listener of every conversation.

And may Heaven's constant benediction crown your union with ever-increasing joy and blessedness, and unite your hearts and lives by the grace and true affection of a happy marriage.

T HE Lord bless you, and keep you; the Lord make his face shine upon you, and be gracious unto you; the Lord lift up his countenance upon you, and give you peace.

The grace of the Lord Jesus Christ, and the love of God, and the communion of the Holy Spirit be with you all. *Amen.*

A SCRIPTURAL SERVICE [1]

Dearly beloved, we are gathered together in the sight of God and in the presence of these witnesses to join together this man and this woman in the bonds of holy matrimony. If there be any here present who knows any just cause why they may not lawfully be joined in marriage, I require him now to make it known, or ever after to hold his peace.

Then shall the minister say to those who are to be married:

The Holy Scriptures set before you the love of Christ for his Church as an example for your devotion. You are not left without guidance concerning the meaning of that love. Hear ye the words of the Apostle:

Love is very patient, very kind;
Love knows no jealousy;
Love makes no parade,

[1] Arranged by Neil Crawford, a Presbyterian minister.

Gives itself no airs,
Is never rude, never selfish;
Never irritated, never resentful.
Love is never glad, when others go wrong.
Love is gladdened by goodness,
Always slow to expose,
Always eager to believe the best,
Always hopeful, always patient;
Love never disappears.

A union embodying such an ideal is not to be entered into lightly or unadvisedly, but reverently, discreetly, advisedly, soberly, and in the fear of God. Into such a union you come now to be joined.

Then shall the minister say:

Do you, _____, take this woman to be your lawful wedded wife, to love and to cherish, to have and to hold; and do you promise, forsaking all others, to cleave to her and to her only so long as you both shall live?

The bridegroom replies:

I do.

Then shall the minister say:

D o you, _____, take this man to be your
lawful wedded husband, to love and to
cherish, to have and to hold; and do you
promise, forsaking all others, to cleave to him
and to him only so long as you both shall live?

The bride replies:

I do.

Then shall the minister say:

Have you a ring?

*The groom shall place the ring on the fourth finger
of the bride's left hand and repeat after the
minister:*

T his ring I give thee in token and pledge of
our constant faith and abiding devotion.

Then shall the minister say:

I nasmuch as you have consented together in
wedlock, and have given and received a
ring in token of your troth, I now declare
you man and wife in the name of Jesus Christ
our Lord.

Then the minister may pray:

G racious Father, thou hast kindled in these
hearts the fire of a divine love. Wilt thou

keep it always aflame upon the altar of their souls. Wilt thou make the inward aspirations of their hearts the outward reality of their home. Wilt thou make that home a place of light and truth, a place of beauty, a place of joy and happiness all the days of their life. *Amen.*

A GOLDEN WEDDING SERVICE

Ministers are frequently asked to participate in the festivities of silver or golden wedding anniversaries. While such occasions are largely social in intent, many desire a religious service for the reconsecration of the principals to the marriage. The following service was written by H. F. Siemsen, Evangelical minister. While created for a golden wedding it is equally useful for the silver anniversary. The ring should be the original wedding ring.

The minister

DEARLY beloved, we are gathered here in the sight of God and in the presence of this company, to help this good man and his dear companion renew the sacred vows which they took *fifty* years ago on this day. This *half* century of happy married life has ripened into a love and loyalty and a devotion that has become a blessing and a benediction to all of us who have learned to know them as friends.

After *fifty* years of happy married life they stand in our presence to bear witness to the fact that marriage is an honorable estate; that it is instituted of God; that it does signify the mystical union between Christ and his Church; that Christ does make married life and home life happy and beautiful and sacred, even as he brought joy and beauty and sacredness into the marriage at Cana of Galilee, which he blessed with his presence.

Yes, with Paul of old, these loved ones are ready to give testimony to the fact that marriage is an honorable thing among all men, and therefore is not to be entered into unadvisedly or lightly, but reverently, discreetly, soberly, and in the spirit of, in the presence of, and in the fear of God. In this holy estate these two persons have lived for *fifty* years, and they come now to renew their covenant, their love, their loyalty, their devotion to each other. In the presence of Christ, who has led them in the midst of joy and difficulty, they give to each other their heart and their hand, all that they have and all that they are.

To the man

fifty years ago you pledged your troth to *N.*, and you took her to be your wedded wife, to live with her after God's ordinance in the holy estate of matrimony. At that time you promised to love her, honor her, cherish her, and keep her in days of good report and in days of evil report. You also promised to be loyal to her whether rich or poor, in sickness or in health. These *fifty* years have found you to be faithful to this pledge. Will you, therefore, now at the close of this *half* century, in the presence of God, *in the presence of your children, in the presence of your grandchildren,* and in the presence of these friends that have gathered here, renew these vows, and continue this devotion to her so long as you both shall live?

Answer

I will.

To the woman

N., *fifty* years ago you pledged your troth to *M.*, and you took him to be your wedded husband, to live with him after God's ordinance in the holy estate of matrimony. At that time you promised to love him, honor him, cherish him, and keep you unto him in days of good report and in days of evil report. You also promised to be loyal to him whether rich or poor, in sickness or in health. These *fifty* years have likewise found you to be faithful to this pledge. Will you, therefore, also, now at the close of this *half* century, in the presence of God, *in the presence of your children, in the presence of your grandchildren*, and in the presence of these friends that have gathered here, renew these vows, and continue this devotion to him so long as you both shall live?

Answer

I will.

To the man

What evidence do you have of this your renewed vow?

The man presents the ring and places it upon the woman's finger, repeating after the minister:

WITH this ring I renew my vow of love and loyalty. With my heart's affection, with my worldly goods I continue thee to endow. In the name of God the Father, the Son, and the Holy Spirit. Amen.

Then they join right hands as the minister says:

FORASMUCH as *M*. and *N*. have renewed their covenant, and have witnessed the same before God and in the presence of this company, and thereto have given their pledge and their troth each to the other, and have declared the same by the giving and the receiving of a ring, and by the joining of their hands, I pray God's blessings and benediction upon them.

Prayer

ALMIGHTY God our heavenly Father, who didst institute the holy estate of matrimony for the mutual help and comfort of thy children; we thank thee that thou hast preserved these thy servants through *fifty* years of married life until this hour. We praise thee for thy goodness to them in making their union one of love, peace, and happiness; and that through thy grace they have been able to keep the vow and covenant betwixt them made. Protect and prosper them, we beseech thee, through the years to come. Multiply thy blessings upon them. May they abound in love and bear together willingly the burdens of life. Encourage and sustain them in all godly living; and may their home continue to be a place of prayer, consecration, and joy. Let thy benediction rest upon them to their life's end, and finally give them a joyful entrance into thy blessed kingdom; through Jesus Christ our Lord. *Amen.*

Benediction

THE Lord bless you and keep you; the Lord make his face shine upon you, and be gracious unto you; the Lord lift up his countenance upon you, and give you peace, now and evermore. *Amen.*

PREMARRIAGE MINISTRY

The normal, functioning church has, in reality, been directing the minds and hearts of its youth toward Christian marriage long before they present themselves before the altar. There have been years of church-school instruction, years of social activity, years of constructive preaching, all of which have sought to aid the individual in developing a healthy attitude toward sex and marriage. These days have been so complicated socially that it has often been difficult to draw definite appraisals of the value of this service. But it may be generally conceded that our daughters are safer with young men who have had religious training and our sons with girls who come out of the Church.

There is a new attitude on the part of the Church toward sex in marriage. Sex suppression is no longer the aim of the religious leader. Rather the social leaders of the Church feel that successful marriages must have a happy physical relationship. The emphasis upon sex in recent religious educational literature is, in itself, evidence of this change.

The wise church will select as its youth leaders

those who have a healthy attitude toward these things. Christian marriage represents the highest social and physical union. Youth should aspire to Christian marriage. The proper kind of social activities will contribute to that end. It is well if the boys and girls of the churches are led to honest conceptions of parenthood and sex relationship through the guidance of the Church.

SERMONS ON MARRIAGE

An increasingly large number of ministers now make it a point to preach sermons dealing with marriage. The canon of the Protestant Episcopal Church makes such preaching obligatory upon its preachers. The canon requires that they "give instruction both publicly and privately, on the nature of Holy Matrimony, its responsibilities and the mutual love and forbearance which it requires." The National Council of the Episcopal Church has distributed among its clergy a booklet containing outlines of sermons dealing with this subject.

The National Council of the Churches of Christ in America points out the need for the Church to take a more aggressive attitude toward marriage problems:

Churches can do much more than they are now doing to lessen the unhappiness and to arrest the collapse of breaking homes. Nobody knows how much unhappiness exists in homes which are outwardly harmonious. It is certainly very great. The chief problems of marriage are subject to educational and spiritual treatment. Every church, at its best, should be a kind of clinic to which people would come for guidance and for help in overcoming their troubles, as they now go to physicians for their physical ills.[1]

PREMARRIAGE INTERVIEWS

The number of ministers who require an interview with the prospective bride and groom is increasing. It is a wise and kindly custom. The earlier the interview the better. If some condition is discovered which would make the union undesirable, the sooner it is known to all parties the better. Many times the minister will act wisely to prevent undesirable marriages—those which must inevitably lead to disease and unhappiness. States which require a period of time to elapse between the application for a marriage license and the marriage itself render a service in this respect. The few days give all parties a chance to think things over.

Much can be done in a sinple interview if the minister has, through reading and experience,

[1] *Ideals of Love and Marriage.* Issued by the Committee on Marriage and the Home of the National Council of the Churches of Christ in America.

prepared himself. Probably he should have a form card for the listing of information desired. Some of the things it should list are:

Nationalities
Ages
Religion
Marriage experience
Intended residence
Income of husband or both
Desire for children and a home
Venereal or transmissible diseases

No minister can hope to be an authority on all the matters mentioned here. But in the community he will find many helpers ready to serve. Many banks will be glad to talk family budgets with the bride and groom. There are social agencies which will advise them regarding their physical conditions. And there are always books which the clergyman can offer to lend. Fortunate is that minister who has so won the respect of his young people that they turn to him as their adviser when they seek information regarding marriage.

The purpose of the pastoral interview is not alone to prevent unfortunate marriages but to help arrange healthy and happy ones. It is not sufficient to find the sources of irritation; that makes the attitude too negative. Instead, try to find out the areas of agreement and understanding which will aid in making the union lasting. Marriage is a normal relationship and no group of citizens should be barred from its joys and responsibilities. The minister consultant should take a positive attitude and seek to aid in making any marriage in which he participates a successful one.

We are in a position of social change which must be recognized in marriage. In many instances it is going to be necessary for both parties to work to maintain the home. It means adjustment so far as children are concerned and social and psychological factors are involved. The clergyman must enter into the picture sympathetically.

One may doubt the wisdom of the average minister's dealing very much, in the premarriage interviews, with the sexual relationship. Place a good booklet in the hands of the couple and let them read it together.[2] The religious nature of marriage should be stressed, and if the couple can be persuaded to unite with the church before the marriage that would be advisable.

The Department of Christian Social Service of the Protestant Episcopal Church offers the

---

[2] See Bibliography in later pages of this Manual.

following outline as the basis for the private instruction of those about to marry:

1. Personality factors:
   Respect for other's personality
   Creative interests: mutual, individual
   Respect for children's personalities
2. Economic factors:
   Danger of existing debts
   Security of income
   Family budgets
   Making of wills
3. Social factors:
   Comparative backgrounds
   The new social unit
   The family in the community
   The state's interest in marriage
4. Sex factors
5. Spiritual factors:
   Sacramental character
   The psychology of permanence
   Spiritual aids

There will be many times when it is a matter of wisdom for the clergyman to refer the couple to some social agency for further consultation. There are such agencies in most counties at the present time. The Planned Parenthood Association of America, Inc., publishes a list of agencies which offer consultation service on maternity, parenthood, and planned births. This list will be sent to any minister upon request. Address the association at 501 Madison Avenue, New York 22, New York.

THE MINISTRY OF BOOKS

There is almost no limit to the list of books now available which touch every phase of this subject. A minister may well have a select list of titles on his own shelves which he can lend to couples who come to him. This loan service is of especial value where sex and birth control are concerned. Many of our young people are not familiar with the good titles which are today available. They have received their sex education from questionable sources. To receive, as a loan, a volume which emphasizes the importance of sex in marriage, from a Christian viewpoint, may mean the shaping of a life of happy marriage. In another section in this book is a fairly complete bibliography on this subject.

THE CONDUCT OF THE WEDDING

Marriage etiquette is founded in history and tradition, so that the minister really has very little to say about it. He should be familiar with the various customs and many times will be called upon to give advice as to the proper procedure. Emily Post is considered an authority in these matters, and he may have occasion to refer to her *Etiquette. The Book of Weddings*, by Mrs. Burton Kingsland, is another volume which will be useful in untangling the knotted threads of wedding plans.

AT THE MINISTER'S RESIDENCE

Many weddings which come to the average minister are unarranged in advance, or arranged by call or telephone a few hours before. The couple, with friends or alone, present themselves at the residence of the minister. In most homes it is understood that the rite of marriage is a serious thing, and the proper privacy is given the minister as he attends to the matter in hand.

The first thing to do is to examine the license to see that it is the regular form. If any question arises as to the conditions under which it has been issued, the minister will do well to satisfy himself in every particular. If the county issues a license to those not qualified to receive it, and the minister has information which leads him to suppose that such is the case, he is morally and legally bound to refuse to honor it.

Satisfied that the license is in legal form, he may then inquire something regarding the individuals. It may be that the law of the state does not synchronize with the law of his Church or his own convictions. He should satisfy himself regarding these things. Then, if the way is clear, he may proceed with the ceremony. If the state law requires witnesses and the parties to be married have provided none, the minister should supply the necessary witnesses.

Clergymen's homes do not usually provide altars for this purpose. A kneeling bench can be constructed, however, which will help out. Most ministers construct their plans so that marriages in their homes are usually solemnized in the same location.

The ceremony itself should be simple. The couple decide whether or not they desire the ring service. They should be instructed regarding the questions which they must answer. Then they take their places together, the woman at the left of the man. Guests or witnesses remain standing during the ceremony. Sometimes the couple bring a best man and a maid of honor to stand with them. In this simple ceremony the best man stands at the right of the man, the maid of honor at the left of the woman.

Many times those who present themselves for this home service have a "let's-get-it-over-with" spirit. The minister should not yield too much to this desire. It is well that he not cut short the introduction to the service nor the prayers. Marriage is a serious proposition, and it is well that the service emphasize its seriousness.

At the conclusion of the benediction the minister may extend his congratulations, first to the bride and then to the groom. Then others present may do so. While they are visiting, the clergyman may complete the certificate, which should be handed to the bride.

From the groom or the best man accompanying the groom the minister receives his honorarium. There is no way of anticipating in advance what this fee may be. It depends upon the wealth and generosity of the groom. After this has been attended to, the newly married couple and their friends drive away—another man and wife on the road of great adventure.

THE CHURCH WEDDING

Some ministers make it a practice to take every marriage into the church, where the ceremony may be performed before the altar. Churches which have small chapels are admirably equipped for this service. Where churches are not continuously heated, this plan, of course, is hardly practicable. Where it is convenient to use the altar of chapel or church, such use is to be commended. It gives the religious atmosphere which should have a part in a Christian marriage.

When the marriage before the altar consists of but the couple and a few friends and witnesses, the procedure is similar to that described in the home. When the church is used for an elaborate wedding, the plan of procedure is different. The wedding then becomes a social event. The plans involve music, ushering, rehearsal, the proper processional, and other things which are considered socially important.

St. Luke's Evangelical Lutheran Church of Chicago has prepared a leaflet of instructions for those who desire to use the church for weddings. Some of the injunctions contained in the leaflet will be of interest to ministers generally. They are worthy of emphasis.

The Church is the House of God; a reverent silence is expected of all who enter here. The members of the congregation should conduct themselves as at any other service. Persons attending weddings and rehearsals are reminded that the House of God is not a place for social functions and that they are expected to conduct themselves reverently and quietly.

No decorations shall be put up before the day of the wedding. No decorations shall be fastened on the woodwork of the chancel or nave. No decorations may be placed in the chancel except the usual palms and vases of flowers for the altar's re-table.

It is in extremely poor taste to follow the heathenish custom of throwing rice or confetti in the church or in front of the building. Please tell your friends that it is forbidden.

Everyone has the right to enter the church and be present throughout the wedding ceremony. The pastor and members of the church boards reserve the right to attend all rehearsals.

Be sure to hand in your license before the ceremony.

The minimum expense for the use of the church is ten dollars aside from fees for the pastor, sexton, organist, and soloist.

Friends and visitors shall remain in their pews at the close of service and give parents and relatives of the bridal party an opportunity to leave.

THE CHURCH PROCESSIONAL

Emily Post says that in the perfect wedding the bride arrives at the church just one minute late. That is to give everybody a chance to be seated. The groom's mother is seated by an usher in the first pew at the right (facing the chancel); the groom's father follows the usher and takes his place beside her. Then the bride's mother is seated in the first pew at the left. This is the signal for the processional. No one is to be seated after the bride's mother takes her seat.

First come the ushers, then the bridesmaids, then the maid (or matron) of honor; flower girls come next, and last of all the bride, leaning on the right arm of her father. The procession moves with deliberation, not too fast, not too slow, with well-measured treads which have probably been carefully practiced. At the foot of the chancel the ushers divide. The first two may, if deemed wise, step up on the first step to the chancel. The bridesmaids divide and take a position in front of the ushers.

While the ushers are walking down the aisle, the minister enters from a door in or near the chancel on the congregation's right and takes his position before the altar (or, in a church with a centered pulpit, usually on the floor in front of the pulpit, though in certain churches it is preferable for the wedding service to be read from the pulpit). He is followed by the bridegroom and his best man, who take their places before him awaiting the bride.

The bride and groom meet in front of the altar. He takes her right hand and draws her right arm through his left, and they step toward the altar and the waiting minister. The father, having released the bride to the groom, stands one step back, still on her left. He keeps this position until that time in the service when the minister asks: "Who giveth this woman to be married?" Then he steps forward, still on her left and halfway between his daughter and the minister but not in front of either; he takes her right hand, which she extends to him, and places it in the hand of the minister. Then the father takes his seat in the pew by the side of his wife.

The ceremony concluded, the minister congratulates the couple, and the recessional begins. The bride takes her bouquet from her maid of honor, turns toward her husband, puts her left hand through his right arm. The bride and groom lead the recessional. The bridesmaids follow, then the ushers. The best man disappears through the door by which he entered to attend to the detail of the minister's fee and then hurries to the bride's home to be of service there.

The ring service is customarily used in church weddings. The bride hands her bouquet to the maid of honor when the ceremony starts so her hand is free for the ring. As the wedding ring is not to be placed over the engagement ring, the engagement ring is either left at home for the marriage ceremony or worn on the right hand.

The best man has the ring in his care. At the proper time he produces it and hands it to the groom. He in turn gives it to the bride, and she passes it to the minister. The minister hands it back to the groom, who places it on the finger of the bride with the proper pledge. If the best man is wise, he has provided himself with a second one, through an arrangement with the jeweler. In the tense moments of the ceremony the ring has often dropped to the floor and defied search. Even if it is located, the quest is not a very dignified procedure. The provision of the second ring will save the situation. The one not used may be returned for credit.

This church service presupposes music, at least for the processional and recessional. If there is a solo, the place for it is just before the ceremony. An address at a wedding is rather unusual in these days, but if given it should come immediately after the first prayer in the service.

MUSIC FOR CHURCH WEDDINGS [1]

Popular music with strong secular overtones, however beautiful in thought, is completely out of context in the church wedding. Reflecting a

[1] Further suggestions for wedding music may be found in the booklet *A Wedding Manual* (Abingdon Press, 1958).

trend toward a more careful selection of instrumental and vocal music for the preservice and services music, the following lists of suitable music are offered:

Processionals (May be used as a congregational hymn)
    "For the Beauty of the Earth" (Dix)
    "Praise, My Soul, the King of Heaven" (Regent Square)
    "Praise the Lord! Ye Heavens, Adore Him" (Hyfrydol)
    "Praise to the Lord" (Lobe Den Herrn)
    "We, Thy People, Praise Thee" (St. Anthony's Chorale)

Recessionals (May be used as a congregational hymn)
    "Joyful, Joyful, We Adore Thee" (Hymn to Joy)
    "Love Divine, All Loves Excelling" (Love Divine)
    "Now Thank We All Our God" (Nun Danket)

Wedding hymns (May be used as an organ or vocal selection)
    "Lord, Who at Cana's Wedding Feast" (St. Leonard)

"May the Grace of Christ Our Saviour"
    (Sardis)
"O Father, All Creating" (Ellacombe)
"O Love Divine and Golden" (Dykes)
"O Perfect Love" (Barnby)
"The King of Love My Shepherd Is" (Dominus Regit Me)

Organ music
Bach, J. S.: "Arioso in A Major"; "Jesu, Joy of Man's Desiring"; "Sheep May Safely Graze"; "Sinfonia from Wedding Cantata"
Franck: "Cantabile"
Handel: Slow Movements from Violin Concertos (Arr.: Klein)
Peters: "Aria"
Sowerby: "Carillon"
Vaughan Williams: "Prelude on 'Rhosymedre'"
Weinberger: "Marriage at Cana in Galilee"

Vocal music:
Bach, J. S.: "Jesus Shepherd, Be Near Me"; "My Heart Ever Faithful"; "O Love That Casts Out Fear"
Chambers: "True Love Is God's Gift"
Dvorak: "The Twenty-third Psalm"; "I Will Sing New Songs of Gladness"
Franck: "O Lord Most Holy"
Handel: "Wedding Hymn"

Lovelace: "A Wedding Benediction"
Willan: "Eternal Love"

THE HOME WEDDING

When the wedding is held in the home of the bride, the same general plan is followed with any adjustments which may be necessary. The bride's mother stands in the door to greet people as they enter, while the groom's parents seat themselves with the other friends.

An improvised altar can be constructed with a kneeling bench. An aisle of white satin and roses reaching from the stairs to this altar may provide the aisle for the bridal party. The minister, groom, and best man come to the altar through a second door. If there is no such door, they may come through the ribbon aisle a few seconds before the bridal party. The bridal party usually comes down the stairs and then to the altar to the strains of music. There is no recessional. As soon as the benediction is pronounced, the group can gather about the newlyweds to extend congratulations. The minister should be the first to greet them.

The officiating minister is expected to remain for the reception, and a prominent place is provided for him at the bride's table. But he should appreciate that the party from this time on belongs to the bride and groom; when the meal is concluded, he should pay his respects to the entertaining parents and gracefully retire.

Sometimes it is desirable that two ministers take part in the marriage service. One is the officiating minister. The legal and moral responsibility for the service rests upon him. The second is invited as a matter of courtesy and is the "assisting minister."

The assistant may have several parts in the service. It is necessary that the officiating minister read the mutual questions, make the pronouncement of marriage, and sign the certificate. He should also give the benedictory prayer at the conclusion. Any of the other parts may be assigned to the assisting minister.

One good division is to have the assisting minister open the service, reading the ritual to the first of the questions asked of the bridal couple. This includes the opening prayer. At that point the service is turned over to the officiating minister. If the assisting minister is to have another part, he may take the prayer at the close of the ceremony. In some services this is followed by the recitation of the Lord's Prayer, and he may then lead the assembly in this prayer.

WHEN A MINISTER BOTH PARTICIPATES AND OFFICIATES

When the daughter of a clergyman marries, the dilemma arises as to whether the minister-parent shall officiate or give the daughter in marriage. In a Cleveland marriage some time ago the problem was met in an interesting way which made it possible for the father to fulfill both functions.

A neighboring minister was asked to assist in the wedding. The bride accompanied her own father to the altar. He acted the part of the parent through the question, "Who giveth this woman to be married to this man?" At that time, having presented the daughter to the assisting minister, he left the wedding party and assumed the part of the officiating minister, asking the questions which followed and making the pronouncement of marriage.

A CONTINUING MINISTRY

The minister who officiates at the wedding will always be remembered by the bride and groom. He should resolve that it will not be the end of a friendly relationship and spiritual service. If the couple are to live in his community, he will seek their relationship to the church. He will have opportunities to help them with their problems of social and financial adjustment. Ministers who have pastorates of long duration always profit by the accumulation of such experiences.

THE MARRIAGE CERTIFICATE

It is customary for the minister to present the bride with a suitable certificate of marriage. A generation ago a large certificate which might be framed and hung on the wall was popular. It later gave way to a wedding booklet. This booklet contained the certificate, several pages of verses and sentiments, with lithographed pictures of flowers, fields, and other scenes. Now the movement appears to be toward an even more simple certificate.

Human tastes vary, of course, but there are

certain tests which may well be made of any marriage certificate. First, it should be attractive but not gaudy. If it is printed in colors, they should be subdued. It is as necessary to avoid hilarity in color as the somberness of mourning. Second, any sentiments which may be expressed should be satisfactory to the minister issuing the certificate. Some publishers issue the same sentiments in their wedding books generation after generation, apparently forgetting that the youth of today live in an era of brazen frankness far removed from the Victorian viewpoint. Some clergymen seek to avoid the obtrusively offensive by using a booklet which contains the marriage service which is used. Others whose resources justify it produce their own booklets. Where there are sufficient marriages to justify the expense this is a desirable practice. However the cost of plates and printing of an attractive wedding booklet is a considerable amount, and most ministers will continue to use services and certificates distributed by the publishing houses. The preference of the writer is for a booklet which contains the service used, but this is purely a personal reaction and not intended to set up a standard.

Irvin Allen Engle uses a well-chosen commercial booklet, but he always adds a personal touch by pasting an additional leaf in the book.

This added leaf may be interesting to other ministers.

This little gift to you is almost valueless from a commercial viewpoint; yet, as it is the token of a happy day, it should be priceless to you as a witness of a pledge of love and loyalty.

Love is of God. Keep God in the home and the coals of love will ever glow on the altars of your hearth. An old and wise philosopher has given to us these practical rules for a happy life:

Never both be angry at once.

Never talk AT one another, either alone or in company.

Never speak loud to one another unless the house is on fire.

Let each one strive to yield oftenest to the wishes of the other.

Let self-denial be the daily aim and practice of each.

Never taunt with a past mistake.

Neglect the whole world besides rather than one another.

Never make a remark at the expense of each other —it is meanness.

Never part for a day without loving words to think of during absence.

Never meet without a loving welcome.

Never let the sun go down upon any anger or grievance.

Never forget the happy hours of early love.

*Never forget that marriage is ordained of God,
and that his blessing alone can make it what it
should be.*

If you make these the rules of your new home,
peace and happiness shall follow you all the days of
your life.

Your officiating minister,
IRVIN ALLEN ENGLE

Theodore Tiemeyer, while pastor of St.
Mark's Evangelical and Reformed Church, New
Albany, Indiana, presented each couple with a
certificate which gives a guarantee of a successful marriage. The copy on the certificate which
follows emphasizes the need of church attend-
ance and pastoral conferences:

Lifetime Guarantee of a Successful Marriage

As pastor of St. Mark's Evangelical and Reformed
Church of New Albany, Indiana, I was highly honored to be granted the privilege of officiating at
your wedding. But my service to you did not end
when the last word of the ritual was spoken. I beg
of you the right to concern myself with the success
of your marriage and your welfare through the
coming years.

My marriage services are guaranteed to bring
about the maximum happiness and the most enduring joy possible. All of this I sincerely wish you.
But there are certain conditions on which my
guarantee is based.

I. This guarantee is valid only if both parties avail themselves of the spiritual guidance and wholesome comradeship which is to be found in regular church worship. In your marriage vows you promised to sustain your devotion not only in time of health, joy, and prosperity, but also in sickness, sorrow, and adversity. Let the church and its fellowship of faith give you strength and courage to face the difficulties which arise in every marriage union.

II. You must also allow spiritual interests to have a vital place in your home life. The use of daily prayer, private devotions, and reading from the Scriptures and other inspirational books is of paramount importance if you hope to retain the original luster of wedded bliss and keep it shining and pure. Make God a guest in your home and your wedded life will take on spiritual height, creative breadth, and an indefinable depth of lasting beauty.

III. My guarantee holds good if you will permit me to be your confidant and adviser. When you need spiritual guidance, moral courage, or social adjustment, or when you need a helping hand, a friendly word, or a sympathetic ear, please feel free to call on me, or on the pastor of your chosen church. Your problems are treated with strictest confidence which even the law cannot force me to betray. I am always ready to help in any possible way.

IV. Please keep me informed of your latest address, that I may keep in contact with you.

My sincerest wish for your continued joy in married life.

THEODORE TIEMEYER

The minister will, of course, keep a record of the marriages he solemnizes. It is well that it be kept in such a form that changes of address may be made as necessary. Even though he may now see no use for this list, it is a matter of detail which may be recognized as worth while. There will come times in the future when he may wish to communicate with individuals or with the entire group. There will be further pastoral service to the members of the group, and occasions will arise when he will wish some kind of record to refresh his memory.

The record of marriages is the property of the church. The minister officiates only as a representative of the church, and the marriage is by the church, not the individual. There is no reason, however, why, in addition to the permanent records of the church, the individual clergyman should not have a personal record of the marriages at which he has officiated.

ANNIVERSARIES

Some preachers make it a point to send some kind of greeting to the couples they have united upon each anniversary of the wedding. It may be simply a post card, but it suffices to call attention to the kind intentions of the minister. Others plan to have one service each year dedicated to those whom they have married. Of course plans for such services must include the children. Invitations sent to all couples married under the present ministry will usually receive a cordial response.

There are other ministers who do not care for the annual reunion, but who do, from time to time, plan special services for all those wedded during their ministry. At this service the sermon may very well be devoted to a discussion of the social problems of home and marriage. It is well if a souvenir booklet of some kind be given to those who attend. If the list of marriages has been carefully kept, it will be an easy matter to get invitations to the entire group.

The following list may be helpful to those who plan to use the anniversaries in keeping in touch with those whom they have married:

First year: paper
Second year: cotton
Third year: leather
Fourth year: books
Fifth year: wooden (clocks)
Sixth year: iron
Seventh year: copper, bronze, or brass

Eighth year: electrical appliances
Ninth year: pottery
Tenth year: tin, aluminum
Eleventh year: steel
Twelfth year: silk or linen
Thirteenth year: lace
Fourteenth year: ivory
Fifteenth year: crystal
Twentieth year: china
Twenty-fifth year: silver
Thirtieth year: pearl
Thirty-fifth year: coral, jade
Fortieth year: ruby
Forty-fifth year: sapphire
Fiftieth year: gold
Fifty-fifth year: emerald
Sixtieth year: diamond

HOME ADJUSTMENTS

If the married couple have an affiliation with the church so that the minister can rightfully do so, he may find opportunity for a constantly growing ministry of guidance in the home. Few married couples get over the first few years without critical days and weeks. A neutral friend with an accumulation of common sense can do a great deal to straighten out the difficulties due to the in-laws, problems of rent, individual friends, and other questions which are sure to arise.

When babies come, he will naturally be called upon for christening and baptism. He may be asked to discuss with one party or the other their own personal habits which threaten to break the faith reposed by the marriage vows. In such cases he must observe rules of propriety to keep away from the accusation of being a snooper. But, led by wisdom and the desire to be of service, the competent minister can render a most valuable spiritual service at this point.

Valuable literature suggestions will be found in the section of this book dealing with bibliography.

PRONOUNCEMENTS OF THE
CHURCHES

Most of the denominations have taken cognizance of the present-day social situation involved in marriage. The increasing number of divorces and the apparent laxity in home loyalties have challenged attention. The excerpts used in this chapter give the views of various church bodies.

THE NATIONAL COUNCIL OF THE CHURCHES OF CHRIST IN THE UNITED STATES OF AMERICA

The following statement on "Safeguarding Marriages" was released by the Committee on Marriage and the Home of the Federal Council and approved by the Executive Committee of the Council. In 1950 it was adopted by the National Council of the Churches of Christ in the U.S.A.

I. *Educational Preparation for Marriage*

Educational preparation for marriage should be given a place in accordance with its great importance. In this education the home, the school, the church and other character-building agencies, and the young people themselves should participate. The instruction given should deal with the principles of happy and successful marriage, such as ideals for the home, wise choice of partners, the wide range of marital adjustments, home management, children and their nurture, and especially with the place of religion in individual and family life.

Pastors have a long-continued opportunity to assist their own people in their preparation for marriage. This assistance can be given by promoting education for home-making as an important part of religious education in the home and the church, also by sermons and lectures, by the use of appropriate literature, by instruction to groups of engaged young couples, and by directing them to further sources of information. To aid in this the pastor may secure material from the proper board of his communion, or from this committee.

II. *Premarital Interviews*

As a part of this preparation for marriage, the Committee believes that pastors have an opportunity to give great help through premarital interviews. Many ministers have done this regularly for years with the most gratifying results. Some hold conferences with the two together, and others separately. These interviews, while frank, should be considerate, and should be guided by circumstances and by the needs of the young persons as they come out in the interview. Through them the minister may assure himself that the marriage is in accordance with the laws of his state and of his church, and that the young people understand the seriousness of the step which they are taking.

Studies in unhappy marriages and the experience of family consultation institutes reveal that ignorance and maladjustment of the sex relationship appear in most cases. The pastor cannot be certain that those who come to him for marriage understand these vital relationships which God himself has ordained and sanctified. If there is inadequate understanding, the pastor may render to the new family a service of the greatest importance through the instruction which he gives them. Literature that will help the young couple in the new adjustments of marriage should be at hand.

Especially will the minister take occasion in these interviews to bring out the religious backgrounds, points of view, associations, and interests of those about to be married; and he will aim to bring the utmost help and inspiration of Christian faith into the life of the new family, knowing that no marriage can rise to the level God intends it to reach except by the assistance of his grace.

III. *The Marriage Ceremony*

Marriages should not be hastily planned nor solemnized by strangers if this can be avoided. Young people should be married by their own pastor, if possible, or by a clergyman in their community. When they are married by a stranger in a strange place, the occasion is robbed of some of the social and spiritual values that ought to be present, and the new home is deprived of the permanent value of the council and fellowship of the minister who has married them.

While weddings may be frequent in the work of a minister, to the young people themselves their own wedding is an event of a lifetime. Therefore, the minister should make it impressive, dignified, and beautiful. He should also encourage simplicity. Above all, he should do all in his power to give it religious significance.

IV. *Commercializing Marriage*

Commercialization of weddings, whether by ministers or civil officials, and degradation of marriage by stunt weddings, by advertising for them, or by using them for advertising purposes, is shocking and antisocial. All of these practices mean that weddings are conducted without sufficient regard for the sacredness of the ceremony, or the spiritual welfare of the persons involved,

and they make improbable either the premarital
instruction or the later pastoral service which the
minister ought to give.

V. *Later Pastoral Service*

Every marriage opens a door of opportunity
to the minister. He has the confidence of the
young people, and they feel that he has had a
vital part in the founding of their home. This
gives him a favorable opportunity to be a spiritual counselor and guide, and to help them in
case difficulties should arise between them. Since
ministers have to deal with the personal problems of their people, they need to engage serious-
ly in the study of methods of personal and family adjustment. Such study will enable them to
raise the level of the marital success of the men
and women whom they marry and of the homes
of their congregations. When newly married
people move to another community, the officiating minister is under obligation to help them
make satisfactory contacts with some church in
the community to which they go.

The Committee recommends the organization
of classes or clubs for young married people in
the churches. In these classes through friendly
association, discussion, reading, or lectures,
homes may be brought to a higher religious level,

and help will come in parent-child relationships, marital adjustments, emotional difficulties, and personality problems.

Both in the personal ministry of the clergyman and in the program of the church, a more definite and intelligent ministry of religion to home life needs emphasis. Above all, in dealing with these delicate and vitally important matters, the minister must work reverently, himself keeping near to God, and securing the best training within his reach.

On Mixed Marriages [1]

Certain principles seem to the Committee on Marriage and the Home to be clear, and the Committee presents the following for consideration:

1. Where the persons contemplating marriage are members of different communions nearly related in doctrine or polity, they may well be advised by their respective pastors to settle the question before marriage by agreeing to attend together one or other of their churches, or even a third church, and to bring up their children in it.

[1] From the leaflet *Intermarriage of Members of Different Christian Communions*, issued by the Committee on Marriage and the Home of the Federal Council. Apparently it was the opinion of the Committee and was offered without official pronouncement of the Council.

2. Where only one of the persons is a member of a church of the Protestant group and the religious differences are profound, such persons should be advised to consider the situation with great seriousness, in all its aspects, and to reach an agreement before marriage.

3. Where intolerable conditions are imposed by either church in which membership is held, persons contemplating a mixed marriage should be advised not to enter it. The Committee on Marriage and the Home protests earnestly against the requirement by any church that the children of mixed marriages should be pledged to that church.

4. Where conferences in the churches interested in the questions arising from mixed marriages can be arranged, such conferences should be welcomed with a view to safeguarding the sanctity of marriage and the spiritual welfare of the home.

THE PROTESTANT EPISCOPAL CHURCH

Marriage with Roman Catholics [1]

RESOLVED, that this Convention earnestly warns members of our Church against contracting marriages with Roman Catholics under the

[1] From a resolution passed at the General Convention of 1949.

conditions imposed by modern Roman Canon Law, especially as these conditions involve a promise to have their children brought up in a religious system which they cannot themselves accept; and, further, because the religious education and spiritual training of their children by word and example is a paramount duty of parents and should never be negleced nor left entirely to others, we assert that in no circumstances should a member of this Church give any understanding, as a condition of marriage, that the children should be brought up in the practice of another communion.

Marriage and Divorce

The Canons of the Church express the doctrine of the Church on Holy Matrimony. According to Canon 18 marriage is a physical, spiritual and mystical union of a man and a woman created by their mutual consent of heart, mind and will thereto and is in intention lifelong. It is further provided by Canon 17 that before solemnizing a marriage a Minister shall require the contracting parties to sign a declaration that they hold marriage to be a lifelong union of husband and wife. Canon 17 provides that no Minister of this Church shall solemnize the marriage of any person who has been the husband or wife of any other person then living whose marriage has been annulled or dissolved by the civil court, except as the Bishop or Ecclesiastical Authority may grant permission on the ground of the existence of one or more of the specific impediments listed in Canon 17 which prevent the existence of a marriage bond as recognized by this Church.

THE METHODIST CHURCH [1]

Marriage Relations

Marriage is an achievement. It doesn't just happen. It comprises a growing oneness in which emotional adjustments from time to time are affected by an understanding of right ways of living together.

a) Preparation. It is increasingly obvious that if marriage is to succeed, there must be adequate preparation. Therefore, it is recommended that a regular course of instruction for youth on the Christian ideals of friendship, courtship, and marriage be given in each local church, using the available materials. In our youth assemblies, camps, and institutes qualified persons should give counsel on personal problems, social relations, and the duties and privileges of Christian marriage. Suitable books, pamphlets, and audio-

[1] Excerpts from the resolutions adopted by the General Conference of The Methodist Church in 1956.

visual resources should be made available for young people. It is further recommended that courses of instruction for young married couples on home building, income budgeting, child training, life adjustments, and personality problems be given by each local church.

The time has come when every person planning marriage should have the opportunity for skilled and careful counseling by ministers or staff workers who are prepared in this field. If this is to be done, pastors must be trained to guide young people through premarital and postmarital counseling.

b) Mixed Marriages. Religious convictions should be a strong tie in marriage. Recent research has emphasized the importance of common cultural and religious backgrounds as the foundations of successful marriage. It is therefore strongly urged that each young person consider carefully before becoming engaged to anyone who does not have a similar religious background. It is important that Protestant youth discuss this problem with their ministers before it is too late. Ministers are urged to discuss with both youth and parents the likelihood of failure in mixed marriages.

c) Planned Parenthood. We believe that planned parenthood, practiced in Christian conscience, may fulfill rather than violate the will of God.

d) Divorce. Divorce is not the answer to the problems that cause it. It is symptomatic of deeper difficulties. The church must stand ready to point out these basic problems to couples contemplating divorce, and help them to discover and, if possible, to overcome such difficulties. In addition, the church must stand ready to depict the unhappy circumstances that are to await the divorced person. As a Christian church, and as ministers, we are obligated to aid, by counsel, persons who have experienced broken marriage, and to guide them so that they may make satisfactory adjustments.

Sex Education. Parents must assume the responsibility of interpreting to each child, before his adolescence, the facts regarding the origin of life. If properly instructed, parents are best fitted to educate their children in regard to sex; but if they have been negligent, then qualified persons in the church should reverently teach the beautiful truths of life. We recognize that sex education is not mere information. It includes also the formation of attitudes and habits.

Legislation. To protect both the individual and society from hasty marriages we favor legislation requiring a period of days or weeks between the application for a marriage license and the granting of it. This will allow sufficient time for consideration on the part of the two persons concerned. We also favor a longer interval between application for and granting of divorce.

We recommend laws requiring a medical examination of both contracting parties, and the refusal of a license to those unfitted physically or mentally by heredity or otherwise for the responsible state of matrimony.

We further favor uniform marriage and divorce laws.

THE AMERICAN BAPTIST CONVENTION

The American Convention through the report of the Council on Christian Social Progress has adopted the following resolutions:

1952—The Family

WHEREAS, the American Baptist Convention has consistently expressed its faith in the home and the family as essential to the foundation of Christlike character and life; and

WHEREAS, the increasing strains and stresses of contemporary life have intensified the need for Christian foundations for the family; and

WHEREAS, the confusion of inconsistent and mutually contradictory federal and state laws contributes to the deplorable fact of increasing divorce in modern society; therefore, be it

Resolved, that we encourage our churches

to adopt premarital counseling and youth programs and institutes, which will guard against mixed marriages, the secularization of marriage and the home, and the blighting evil of divorce. Furthermore, be it

Resolved, that we urge our people to establish the practice of a daily family altar in every American Baptist home. Furthermore, be it

Resolved, that we support the enactment of federal and state laws which will bring consistency and uniformity in the marriage and divorce laws of our nation.

1953—Marriage and Family Life

WHEREAS, There are many destructive influences at work in our society which weaken the moral structure and unity of the family, and which make it difficult for the family to function as a unit of Christian growth where Christ is loved and honored, and

WHEREAS, A growing number of Christian people are resorting to the legal processes of divorce as a method of solving problems of marital and family discord, and

WHEREAS, a growing number of Christian couples are entering into the holy bonds of marriage without the benefits of premarital counseling or instruction in preparation for Christian marriage, and

WHEREAS, family worship in Christian homes is widely neglected, and

WHEREAS, family life education within the church is often disregarded as an integral part of the total program of education and fellowship; therefore, be it

Resolved, that we call upon all who plan and administer programs which relate to Christian marriage and family life in American Baptist churches to become more aggressive in developing activities that will inspire and motivate church leaders, parents and family groups through such emphases as premarital instruction, family-centered church programs, family worship and Christian living in the home.

1954—Marriage and Family Life

We recommend more attention to the planning and administering of programs relating to Christian marriage and family life. We urge all pastors to adopt the practice of premarital counseling.

We strongly recommend to all our churches the use of American Baptist home-related literature and the promotion of family worship including mealtime grace and regular home Bible reading and prayer.

Foster Homes for Needy Children

We encourage the members of the churches of our Convention to open their homes to foster children as the best means of caring for homeless and needy boys and girls. We recognize this as one of the finest kinds of Christian service, a means of providing Christian nurture and preventing possible delinquency.

Homes for the Aged

Recognizing the increasing problems of the older members of our churches and communities, we urge active participation by our churches in planning for the welfare of the aging, and we encourage the establishment of adequate homes in areas where they are needed.

1955—Family Problems

Recognizing the increasing problems that come from broken homes, and realizing that homeless children may easily become delinquent, we call attention to the need for pastoral counseling and the necessity of helping parents and children to make those adjustments that will save both parents and children from frustration and family disintegration. For this reason we recommend that pastors familiarize themselves with the techniques and practices of Christian counseling, and set apart certain periods of the week for this purpose. We recommend to our people the literature and help our denomination is providing in the field of juvenile protection.

Summary Statements on Marriage and Family Life

1. Marriage is that order of creation given by God in love which binds one man and one woman in a life-long union of the most intimate fellowship of body and life. This one-flesh relation, when properly based on fidelity and love, serves as a witness to God's grace and leads husband and wife into service one of the other. In their marriage, husband and wife are responsible to God for keeping their vows and must depend upon his love and mercy to fulfill them.

2. God has established the sexual relation for the purpose of bringing husband and wife into full unity so that they may enrich and be a blessing to each other. Such oneness, depending upon life-long fidelity between the marriage partners and loving service one of the other, is the essential characteristic of marriage. Marriage should be consummated in love with the intention of maintaining a permanent and responsible relation. Continence outside of marriage and fidelity within marriage are binding on all.

---

[1] Taken from a summary of statements on marriage and family life which appear in an attractive thirty-page leaflet entitled *Christian Guidance on Marriage and Family Life.* These statements are a declaration of a convention of the United Lutheran Church in America.

3. Procreation is a gift inherent in the sex relation. In children the one-flesh idea finds embodiment. Children bring great joy to marriage and reveal how God permits men to share in his continuing creation. Married couples should seek to fulfill their responsibilities in marriage by conceiving and nurturing their children in the light of Christian faith.

4. Husband and wife are called to exercise the power of procreation responsibly before God. This implies planning their parenthood in accordance with their ability to provide for their children and carefully nurture them in fullness of Christian faith and life. The health and welfare of the mother-wife should be a major concern in such decisions. Irresponsible conception of children up to the limit of biological capacity and selfish limitation of the number of children are equally detrimental. Choice as to means of conception control should be made upon professional medical advice.

5. Marriage, as ordained by God, is a life-long indissoluble union consummated through consent and coitus. Any breaking of the marriage bond involves sin and suffering. Forgiveness and reconciliation are incumbent upon all within marriage, and especially upon Christians. The church should extend its counseling services in an effort

to maintain and strengthen families when they face difficulties threatening their unity.

6. Where marriage failure and divorce occur among Christian people, the church should recognize its involvement in the failure and seek to lead all concerned to repentance and forgiveness. If it proves impossible or unwise in the light of Christian love and concern for the welfare of all involved to reconstitute the marriage, then the church should continue, insofar as possible, to minister to each person involved.

If the question of the remarriage of a divorced person arises, pastors and congregations of The United Lutheran Church in America should make their decisions on the particular circumstances in each case, being guided by the following considerations:

a) While it is the Christian teaching that marriage is a life-long, indissoluble union and that divorce and remarriage do violate God's order, nevertheless, God in his love does accept the sinner and deals with him according to his need. The church has recognized that marriage may be a remedy for sin and has seen in such Bible passages as Matthew 5:32, 19:9, and I Corinthians 7:15 the possibility of remarriage, but it also knows that the final basis of decision is loving concern for man in his actual situation.

b) The divorced person seeking remarriage

must recognize his responsibility in the breakup of the former marriage. He must give evidence of repentance and have made an effort to overcome his limitations and failures. He must have forgiven his partner in the former marriage, and he and his intended spouse must give assurance that he will fulfill his obligations to those involved in his former marriage.

c) The divorced person must give evidence of his Christian faith by his witness in the church and must have received adequate counsel and training in preparation for marriage. He must be prepared to undertake the full responsibilities of marriage in dependence upon God.

7. The church should provide opportunities for its pastors and lay leaders to prepare themselves to meet their responsibilities in ministering to families and young people contemplating marriage. This involves seminary training, in-service training opportunities, college courses, and special courses and institutes for lay leaders. Study material based on the view of marriage set forth in these *Summary Statements* should be provided.

8. Congregations should provide opportunities for study courses and other activities in preparation for marriage. Help should be given through activities strengthening and enriching the life of existing family groups. Each pastor should re-

quire regular counseling periods with couples before marriage. In part this may be done with groups, but private and individual conferences should also be required.

THE UNITED PRESBYTERIAN CHURCH IN THE UNITED STATES OF AMERICA [1]

From the Confession of Faith, Chapter XXIV, Sections 1 and 2

1. Christian marriage is an institution ordained of God, blessed by our Lord Jesus Christ, established and sanctified for the happiness and welfare of mankind, into which spiritual and physical union one man and one woman enter, cherishing a mutual esteem and love, bearing with each other's infirmities and weaknesses, comforting each other in trouble, providing in honesty and industry for each other and for their household, praying for each other, and living together the length of their days as heirs of the grace of life.

2. Because the corruption of man is apt unduly to put asunder those whom God hath joined together in marriage and because the Church is concerned with the establishment of marriage in the Lord as Scripture sets it forth,

[1] From a statement by Eugene Carson Blake, Stated Clerk of the General Assembly, under date of September 28, 1953.

and with the present penitence as well as with the past innocence or guilt of those whose marriage has been broken; therefore as a breach of that holy relation may occasion divorce, so remarriage after a divorce granted on grounds explicitly stated in Scripture or implicit in the gospel of Christ may be sanctioned in keeping with his redemptive gospel, when sufficient penitence for sin and failure is evident, and a firm purpose of and endeavor after Christian marriage is manifest.

Directory for Worship, Chapter XIV, Sections 9, 10, and 11

9. The minister should keep a proper register of the names of all whom he marries and of the time of their marriage for the perusal of all whom it may concern, and a duplicate copy of this register should be a part of the permanent records of the church. Ministers without charge should also maintain such a register, and furnish a duplicate of the certificate to the officers of the appropriate church. There should be at least two witnesses present at the solemnization of the marriage, and a certificate of the marriage, signed by the officiating minister and the witnesses, should be given to the contracting parties.

10. Inasmuch as the Church must uphold the Christian home and the permanence of the mar-

riage tie, and at the same time minister sympathetically to any who have failed in this holy relation, ministers who are requested to remarry divorced persons shall ascertain whether there is penitence for past sin and failure, and intention to enter, with the help of God, and through His Church, into a marriage of love, honor, forbearance, and loyalty, which will continue as long as both shall live.

To implement the opposition of the Church to hasty remarriage, a minister shall officiate at the remarriage of a divorced person only after a period of at least one year has elapsed from the date of the granting of the divorce, except with the approval of presbytery or its authorized representative.

In the interests of Christian comity, ministers are advised not to unite in marriage a member of any other Christian communion whose marriage is known to the minister to be prohibited by the laws of the Church in which such person holds membership, unless the minister believes that his refusal would do injustice.

11. Since marriage confers the blessing of the Church, its solemnization lays upon ministers of the Church a weighty responsibility. In cases where the interpretation of the law of the Church is in doubt, ministers are entitled to the aid and counsel of their brethren in session and presby-

tery. To provide such aid and counsel, each presbytery may elect a Committee on Christian Marriage.

When a minister seeks the counsel of presbytery as to a proposed marriage or remarriage, he shall submit all the papers and facts in the case, including his considered judgment, to presbytery or its authorized representative, which shall be judge of satisfactory evidence as to whether there are grounds for marriage or remarriage in keeping with the spirit and teachings of our Lord, Jesus Christ. The decision of presbytery shall be made a matter of record.

THE EVANGELICAL AND REFORMED CHURCH

The Church's Teaching on Marriage and Divorce [1]

The pastoral obligation of the Church includes:

A. Definite presentation of Christian standards on marriage and the family by (1) preaching, (2) instruction of confirmands, of young people, and of adults in catechetical and church school classes, and (3) articles in ecclesiastical publications, pamphlets, and books.

B. Conferences between the pastor and parties

[1] As adopted by the General Synod of the Evangelical and Reformed Church in 1944.

to a marriage before the marriage ceremony so that no marriage ceremony be performed without the contracting parties having a clear understanding of the nature and obligation of Christian marriage and Christian family life. The rubric in the "Order for Marriage" in the *Book of Worship* states, "It shall be the duty of the minister to confer beforehand with the contracting parties, counseling them in the meaning of Christian marriage."

C. An alertness on the part of both ministry and members to warn against and, if possible, remove conditions or influences subversive of the best interests of the family.

The following practices should be discouraged:

1. Marrying couples whose only qualification is possession of a marriage license.

2. Marrying couples who are connected with some other charge, with no valid reason for not being married by the pastor of the congregation with which they are connected. (See paragraph 35 of the Bylaws of the Evangelical and Reformed Church.)

3. Solemnizing marriages in settings which because they are bizarre, or vulgar, or ostentatious displays of wealth, or some like reason, detract from the reverence appropriate to such an occasion.

The following practices should be encouraged:

1. Special instruction for engaged couples in the nature and meaning of marriage before the day of the wedding, by the pastor by way of personal counseling and making available helpful literature. (L. Foster Woods, *Harmony in Marriage*, is a booklet which can be heartily recommended.)

2. A waiting period between public declaration of intention to marry—for example, issuance of the marriage license by civil authority—and the marriage rite.

3. A health examination, prior to marriage, of both parties.

In cases where one or both parties to the marriage have been divorced, the minister asked to officiate should satisfy himself by conference with the parties and such investigation as may be necessary that:

1. The divorced party or parties to the marriage have given evidence of sincere repentance.

2. There has been a decent interval of time —at least one year—between the granting of the divorce decree and the issuance of the license for the second marriage.

3. The conditions leading to the former dissolution are not, as far as can be ascertained, present in the intended union.

Inter-Faith Marriages [2]

The following guiding principles are suggested as helpful:

1. Pastors and lay leaders should consider it a special duty to assist every confirmand and member to gain an intelligent understanding of the positive teachings of Protestant Christianity and of the essential differences between that and Roman Catholicism.

2. Parents and local church leaders should co-operate in counseling with youth concerning the problems involved in inter-faith marriages during times of friendship, dating, and courtship.

3. Our young people should be helped to understand that marriages whether performed by Protestant or Roman Catholic clergy are valid in law and before God; and that the superior authority claimed by the Roman clergy and stressed by the Roman Church is an usurpation of the authority which belongs to Christ alone.

Since equal freedom of action is a requisite for mutuality in love and affection, people of different faiths are more likely to effect godly marriages through Protestant rites in which this freedom is kept inviolate than through Roman Catholic rites which deprive one of the contract-

---

[2] As adopted by the General Synod of the Evangelical and Reformed Church in 1953.

ing parties of freedom where this is most essential.

The response God asks of us is a response *freely* given. And in His service we find our freedom. To deny spiritual freedom to others is a grave offense. Hence the effort to restrict by "contracts" the freedom of persons—and, much more, the Spirit of God—is mistaken and wrong. We testify to our conviction that it is by placing ourselves under the Word of God and by being guided by the Holy Spirit who leads us into all truth that we find Him who is the Way and the Truth and the Life.

A BIBLIOGRAPHY ON MARRIAGE

FOR THE PASTOR

Cole, William Graham. *Sex in Christianity and Psycho-analysis*. New York: Oxford University Press, 1955.

Dicks, Russell L. *Pastoral Work and Personal Counseling*. New York: The Macmillan Co., 1949.

Doherty, Joseph. *Moral Problems of Interracial Marriage*. Washington, D.C.: Catholic University of America, 1950.

Groves, Ernest R. *Christianity and the Family*. New York: The Macmillan Co., 1942.

Hedley, George R. *The Minister Behind the Scenes*. New York: The Macmillan Co., 1956.

Hiltner, Seward. *Pastoral Counseling*. Nashville: Abingdon Press, 1949.

Kemp, Charles F. *Physicians of the Soul: A History of Pastoral Counseling*. New York: The Macmillan Co., 1947.

Mace, David. *Success in Marriage*. Nashville: Abingdon Press, 1958.

Maves, Paul B. ed. *The Church and Mental Health*. New York: Charles Scribner's Sons, 1953.

May, Rollo. *The Art of Counseling*. Nashville: Abingdon Press, 1939.

Oates, Wayne E. *Where to Go for Help*. Philadelphia: Westminster Press, 1957.

Pike, James A. *If You Marry Outside Your Faith*. New York: Harper & Bros., 1954.

Wise, Carroll A. *Pastoral Counseling. Its Theory and Practice*. New York: Harper & Bros., 1951.
The Pastor's Manual for Premarital Counseling. Nashville: The Methodist Publishing House, 1958.

FOR THOSE ABOUT TO MARRY

Adams, Theodore F. *Making Your Marriage Succeed*. New York: Harper & Bros., 1953.

Bailey, Derrick S. *The Mystery of Love and Marriage*. New York: Harper & Bros., 1952.

Brink, Frederick W. *This Man and This Woman*. New York: Association Press, 1948.

Butterfield, Oliver M., *Sexual Harmony in Marriage*. New York: Emerson Books, Inc., 1953.

Duvall, Evelyn M., and Hill, Reuben. *When You Marry*. Rev. ed. New York: Association Press, 1953.

Duvall, Sylvanus M. *Men, Women, and Morals*. New York: Association Press, 1953.

Hiltner, Seward. *Sex and the Christian Life*. New York: Association Press, 1957.

Landis, Judson T. and Mary G. *The Marriage Handbook*. Englewood Cliffs, N. J.: Prentice-Hall, Inc., 1953.

Maynard, Donald M. *Looking Toward Christian Marriage*, Nashville: Abingdon Press, 1958.

Stone, Hannah M. and Abraham. *A Marriage Manual*. Rev. ed. New York: Simon & Schuster, Inc., 1952.

Wood, Leland Foster and Dickinson, R. L. *Harmony in Marriage*. New York: Round Table Press, 1939.

In Holy Matrimony. Nashville: The Methodist Publishing House, 1958.

FOR PARENTS

Bossard, James H. S. *Parent and Child*. Philadelphia: University of Pennsylvania Press, 1953.

Brown, Alberta Z. *Teens to 21*. St. Louis, Mo.: Bethany Press, 1957.

Cady, Ernest and Francis. *How to Adopt a Child*, New York: Whiteside, Inc., 1956.

Chaplin, Dora P. *Children and Religion*. New York: Charles Scribner's Sons, 1948.

Gebhard, Anna Laura and Edward W. *Guideposts to Creative Family Worship*. Nashville: Abingdon Press, 1953.

Groves, Ernest R. *Conserving Marriage and the Family*. New York: The Macmillan Co., 1944.

Jones, Mary Alice. *Guiding Children in Christian Growth*. Nashville: Abingdon Press, 1949.

Mace, David R. *Marriage: The Art of Lasting Love*. New York: Doubleday & Co. 1952.

Maynard, Donald M. *Your Home Can Be Christian*. Nashville: Abingdon Press, 1952.

McKim, Judson J. *The Formal Wedding*. Westwood, N. J.: Fleming H. Revell Co., 1947.

Parkhurst, Helen. *Exploring the Child's World*. New York: Appleton-Century-Croft, Inc., 1951.

Piper, Otto A. *The Christian Interpretation of Sex*. New York: Charles Scribner's Sons, 1941.

Wynn, John Charles. *How Christian Parents Face Family Problems*. Philadelphia: The Westminster Press, 1955.

STATE LAWS ON MARRIAGE

The laws regarding marriage are under the authority of the various states; marriage is not, in itself, a federal affair. Social reformers have dreamed of uniform laws on marriage and divorce, but that has not yet been achieved. It is obvious, however, that the various states are moving toward such a practice. During the past generation we have seen the passing from unlicensed marriage to a system of licensing. There is no state in the union now where a clergyman or any other official may officiate at a wedding unless the couple brings a license issued by the proper authority.

It is also noticeable that there is a trend toward requiring blood tests (Wassermann or its equivalent), their being required in all but five of the states and the District of Columbia. These states are Maryland, Minnesota, Nevada, South Carolina, and Washington. The new states, Alaska and Hawaii require the blood test. The Canal Zone, Guam, Puerto Rico, and the Virgin Islands do not.

Many states require a waiting period between the application for a license and the issuing of it. Four states—Delaware, Louisiana, New York, and Vermont—require a waiting period between the issuance of the license and the marriage.

Most states recognize common law marriages.

The ceremony of the Friends tradition is permitted in some states, and no civil authority or minister is required. Some will recognize contract marriages if they are properly witnessed. Maryland is the only state which does not recognize civil marriages.

In officiating at a marriage, the minister becomes an officer of the state and must comply with the qualifications demanded of the state before he is authorized to function in this way. Some states require registry; some make more serious demands. Some insist on surety bonds. In moving from one state to another, the clergyman should always seek to find out what credentials he must present to qualify for this service.

The laws concerning consanguinity may be confusing [1] because in different states they are based on different codes. Some have their origin in civil law, some in canonical law, some in common law. In all cases the degrees of lineal relationship are the same. One's child is a relation of the first degree, a grandchild is a relation of the second degree, and so on; but there are two methods of computing degrees of collateral relationship. Under civil law the degree of collateral relationship is the sum of the degrees of lineal relationship of both parties to a common ancestor. By this reckoning, one's sister is related in the second degree; one's aunt in the third degree; one's first cousin in the fourth degree. Under canon law and common law the degree of

---

[1] Compare the laws of the ancient Hebrews found in the eighteenth and twentieth chapters of Leviticus.

collateral relationship is the same as the degree of lineal relationship of one party to the common ancestor—the more remote if there is a difference. By thus reckoning, one's sister is related in the first degree, the same as one's mother, while one's aunt or first cousin is related in the second degree, the same as one's grandmother.

Some states forbid marriage within certain degrees of affinity (relationship to blood relatives of a spouse). In most cases the prohibitions apply only to the ancestors or descendants of the former spouse.

In the following outline, to avoid confusion of the differing methods of computation, the specific relatives a man may not marry are usually named; it should be understood that a woman may not marry the corresponding male relatives.

The racial restrictions will be more easily understood. They follow the state concepts on racial integration. Most southern states prohibit marriage between blacks and whites. One state will not permit a black minister to officiate at a white wedding. Other states prohibit marriage between whites and Indians. California prohibits the marriage of whites to blacks, mulattoes, browns, and yellows.

While the reported laws place age limits for marriage, the courts of the states have the right to permit marriage at earlier age than those listed when it seems that the marriage is desirable for moral or humane considerations. This is frequently the practice in the case of pregnancy.

ALABAMA

License issued by probate judge of county in which woman resides or in which ceremony is to be performed. Cost of license, $2.00. Minimum ages: male, 17; female, 14. Parental consent necessary when male is under 21, female under 18. No marriage of male venereals. Blood test required. No marriage between blacks and whites. Man is not permitted to marry mother, daughter, granddaughter, sister, half sister, aunt, niece, half niece, stepmother, son's widow, stepdaughter, or wife's granddaughter.

ALASKA

Cost of license, $2.50. Waiting period for license, 3 days. No waiting period necessary after issuance. Minimum ages: male, 18; female, 16. Parental consent necessary when male is under 21, female under 18. Blood test required.

ARIZONA

License issued by clerk of superior court in county in which one of parties resides or in which marriage is to take place. Cost of license, $2.00. Minimum ages: male, 18; female, 16. Parental consent necessary when male is under 21, female under 18. Blood test required. Whites may not marry blacks, reds, or yellows. Man is not permitted to marry mother, daughter, grandmother, granddaughter, sister, half sister, aunt, niece, first cousin.

ARKANSAS

License issued by clerk of county court of any county in the state. Cost of license, $3.00. Waiting period for license, 3 days. Minimum ages: male, 18; female, 16. Parental consent necessary when male is under 21, female under 18. Blood test required. Minister must have certificate from clerk of county authorizing him to perform marriages. No marriages between whites and blacks or mulattoes. Man may not marry mother, daughter, grandmother, granddaughter, sister, half sister, aunt, niece, first cousin.

CALIFORNIA

License issued by county clerk of county in which marriage is to be solemnized. Cost of license, $2.00. Minimum ages; male, 18; female, 16. Parental consent necessary when male is under 21, female under 18. Blood test required within thirty days of ceremony. One witness required. Whites cannot marry blacks, mulattoes, browns, or yellows. No marriage of imbeciles, insane, drunkards, or narcotics. Man is not permitted to marry mother, daughter, grandmother, granddaughter, sister, aunt, niece.

COLORADO

License issued by any county clerk. Cost of license, $2.00. Minimum ages; male, 16; female, 16. Parental consent necessary male is under 21, female under 18. Blood test required. No marriages between blacks or mulattoes and whites. Man cannot marry mother, daughter, grandmother, grand-daughter, sister, half sister, aunt, niece, half niece, or first cousin. This latter restriction does not prohibit persons living in sections of the state acquired from Mexico from marrying in accordance with the old Mexican custom.

CONNECTICUT

License issued by registrar of births, marriages, and deaths of town in which marriage is to be celebrated. Cost of license, $2.00. Waiting period for license, 5 days. Minimum ages: both sexes, 16 years. Parental consent necessary when under 21. Blood test required. No marriage of epileptics or feeble-minded. No racial restrictions. Man may not marry mother, daughter, grandmother, granddaughter, sister, aunt, niece, stepmother, stepdaughter.

DELAWARE

License issued by clerk of peace of county or local magistrate. Cost of license, $3.00. Local justice cannot issue license for minor, divorcee, patient or former patient of insane asylum, or person on parole; these licenses must be issued by clerks of peace or their deputies. Ninety-six hours must elapse after license is issued in case of nonresidents; 24 when one party is a resident. Minimum ages: male, 18; female, 16. Parental consent necessary when male is under 21, female under 18. Blood test required. Two witnesses necessary. No marriage between whites and blacks. No marriage of epileptics,

venereals, drunkards, insane, narcotics, or those suffering from a communicable disease. Man must not
marry mother, daughter, grandmother, granddaughter, sister, aunt, niece, first cousin.

DISTRICT OF COLUMBIA

License issued by the clerk's office of supreme
court of the District of Columbia. Cost of license:
50¢ on application; $2.00 when license is issued.
Waiting period for license, 3 days. Minimum ages:
male, 18; female, 16. Parental consent necessary
when male is under 21, female under 18. No blood
test required. Minister must be authorized by a
justice of supreme court of the district. No racial
restrictions. No marriage of idiot or lunatic. Man
cannot marry mother, daughter, grandmother,
granddaughter, sister, aunt, niece, stepmother,
daughter-in-law, grandfather's wife, grandson's
wife, mother-in-law, stepdaughter, wife's grandmother, wife's granddaughter.

FLORIDA

License issued by judge of county in which woman resides. Cost of license, $3.00. Waiting period
for license, 3 days. Minimum ages: male, 18; female,
16. Parental consent necessary when under 21.
Blood test required. White cannot marry black.
One-eighth Negro blood is sufficient to make person legally a black. Man cannot marry mother,
daughter, grandmother, granddaughter, sister, aunt,
niece.

GEORGIA

License issued by ordinary of county where female resides; if she is nonresident, by ordinary of county where ceremony is to be performed. Cost of license, $5.00. Waiting period for license, 5 days. Minimum ages: male, 17; female, 14. Parental consent necessary when male is under 21, female under 18. Blood test required. Black ministers to marry blacks only. White cannot marry black. Man cannot marry mother, daughter, grandmother, granddaughter, sister, aunt, niece, stepmother, daughter-in-law, mother-in-law, stepdaughter, wife's granddaughter.

HAWAII

Cost of license, $3.00. Waiting period for license, 3 days. Minimum ages: male, 18; female, 16. Parental consent necessary when under 20. Blood test required.

IDAHO

License issued by county recorder of any county. Cost of license, $3.00. Minimum age for both male and female, 15. Parental consent necessary when under 18. Blood test required. Whites may not marry blacks or mulattoes. Man may not marry mother, daughter, grandmother, granddaughter, sister, half sister, aunt, niece, first cousin.

ILLINOIS

License issued by county clerk of county where marriage is to be solemnized. (Term interchangeable witth "clerk of the county court.") Members of Society of Friends exempted from this provision. Cost of license: Cook County, $5.00; balance of state, $1.00. Minimum ages; male, 18; female, 16. Parental consent necessary when male is under 21, female under 18. Blood test required. No statutes prohibiting interracial marriages. No marriage of insane or idiots. Man may not marry mother, daughter, grandmother, granddaughter, sister, half sister, aunt, niece, grandaunt, great-grandaunt, first cousin.

INDIANA

License issued by clerk of circuit court of county in which female resides. Cost of license, $3.00. Waiting period for license, 3 days. Members of Society of Friends are exempted from necessity of license. Minimum ages: male, 18; female, 16. Parental consent necessary when male is under 21, female under 18. Blood test required. White person may not marry one having one-eighth or more Negro blood. No marriage of imbeciles, epileptics, insane, narcotics, drunkards, or those suffering from transmissible disease. Man may not marry mother, daughter, grandmother, granddaughter, sister, aunt, niece, grandaunt, great-grandaunt, first cousin, grandniece, great-grandniece, first cousin once removed.

IOWA

License issued by clerk of district court of county where marriage will be solemnized. Cost of license,

$3.00. Minimum ages: male, 16; female, 14. Parental consent necessary when male is under 21, female under 18. Blood test required. No racial provisions. No marriage of imbeciles, insane, or epileptics. Man may not marry mother, daughter, grandmother, granddaughter, sister, aunt, niece, first cousin, stepmother, son's widow, grandson's widow, mother-in-law, stepdaughter.

KANSAS

License issued by probate judge of any county. Cost of license, $2.50 plus $1.00 registration fee. Waiting period for license, 3 days. Quakers exempted from necessity of license. Minimum ages: male, 18; female, 16. Parental consent necessary when male is under 21, female under 18. Blood test required. No racial provisions. No marriage of epileptics, feeble-minded, or insane unless woman is over forty-five. Man may not marry mother, daughter, grandmother, granddaughter, sister, half sister, aunt, niece, first cousin.

KENTUCKY

License issued by clerk of county in which female resides. Cost of license, $6.00. Waiting period for license, 3 days. Minimum ages: male, 16; female, 14. Parental consent necessary when under 21. Blood test required. Minister must obtain license from court of county in which he resides. Two witnesses required. Whites may not marry blacks or mulattoes. No marriage of idiots or insane. Man may not marry mother, daughter, grandmother, granddaughter, sister, aunt, niece, grandniece, stepmother, stepdaughter, grandfather's wife, grandson's wife, mother-in-law, daughter-in-law, wife's grandmother, wife's granddaughter. Prohibition in these cases stands whether relationship is dissolved by death or by divorce.

LOUISIANA

Licenses in New Orleans issued by board of health and judges of city courts; in other parishes by clerks of courts. Cost of license, $2.00. Waiting period of 72 hours after license is issued. Minimum ages: male, 18; female, 16. Parental consent necessary when under 21. Blood test required. Three witnesses required. Whites may not marry persons of color. Man may not marry mother, daughter, grandmother, granddaughter, sister, half sister, aunt, niece, first cousin.

MAINE

Certificate of intention to marry must be filed with town clerk of town in which each resides, or in town where marriage is to be celebrated. Cost of license, $2.00. Waiting period for license, 5 days. Minimum ages: male and female, 16. Parental consent necessary when male is under 21, female under 19. Blood test required. Minister must have certificate from secretary of state authorizing him to officiate. Two witnesses required. No racial provisions. No marriage of venereals, insane, idiots, or feeble-minded. Man may not marry mother, daughter, grandmother, granddaughter, sister, aunt, niece, stepmother, son's wife, grandfather's wife, grandson's wife, wife's mother, wife's daughter, wife's grandmother, wife's granddaughter.

MARYLAND

License issued by clerk of circuit court in county where marriage is to take place. Cost of license, $3.00 to $6.00 depending on county. Waiting period for license, 48 hours. Church banns necessary on three Sundays. Quakers exempted from license provision. Minimum ages: male, 18; female, 16. Parental consent necessary when male is under 21, female under 18. No blood test required. No civil marriage in Maryland. No marriage of whites with blacks or browns. Man may not marry mother, daughter, grandmother, granddaughter, sister, aunt, niece, stepmother, stepdaughter, grandfather's wife, grandson's wife, mother-in-law, daughter-in-law, wife's grandmother, wife's granddaughter.

MASSACHUSETTS

Certificate of intention to be filed with clerk or registrar of town where either party resides; if nonresidents, in town where ceremony is to be performed, at least five days before the marriage. Cost of license, $2.00. Waiting period for license, 5 days. Minimum ages: male, 14; female, 12. Parental consent necessary when male is under 18, female under 16. Blood test required. No racial restrictions.

Insane persons incapable of contracting marriage. Man may not marry mother, daughter, grandmother, granddaughter, sister, aunt, niece, stepmother, daughter-in-law, grandfather's w i f e, mother-in-law, stepdaughter, wife's granddaughter. Prohibition stands whether relationship is dissolved by death or by divorce.

MICHIGAN

License issued by county clerk of county in which either party lives; if nonresident, in county in which ceremony is to be solemnized. Cost of license, $2.00. Waiting period for license, 3 days. Minimum ages: male, 18; female, 16. Parental consent necessary when under 21. Blood test required. No racial restrictions. Two witnesses required. Marriage of venereals, idiots, epileptics, or insane not permitted. Man may not marry mother, daughter, grandmother, granddaughter, sister, aunt, niece, stepmother, daughter-in-law, grandfather's wife, grandson's wife, mother-in-law, stepdaughter, wife's grandmother, wife's granddaughter.

MINNESOTA

License issued by clerk of district court of county in which woman resides; if nonresident, from clerk of court where marriage is to be solemnized. Cost of license, $3.00. Waiting period for license, 5 days. Minimum ages: male, 16; female, 15. Parental consent necessary when male is under 18, female under 16. No blood test required. Ministers must have certificate from clerk of district court of some county in state. Two witnesses required. No racial restrictions. No marriage of epiletics, feeble-minded, idots, or insane. Marriages between persons nearer of kin than second cousins prohibited. Man may not marry mother, daughter, grandmother, granddaughter, sister, aunt, niece, grandaunt, great-grandaunt, first cousin, grandniece, great-grandniece.

MISSISSIPPI

License issued by clerk of circuit court of county in which female usually resides. Cost of license, $3.00. Waiting period for license, 3 days. Minimum ages: male, 17; female, 15. Parental consent necessary when male is under 21, female under 18. Blood test required. No marriage between white and black, mulatto, or yellow. No marriage of insane or idiots. Man may not marry mother, daughter, grandmother, granddaughter, sister, half sister, aunt, niece, first cousin, stepmother, son's widow, stepdaughter, wife's granddaughter.

MISSOURI

License issued by county recorder, or recorder of the city of St. Louis. Cost of license, $2.55. Waiting period for license, 3 days. Minimum ages: male, 15; female, 15. Parental consent necessary when male is under 21, female under 18. Blood test required. No marriage between whites and blacks or yellows. No marriage of insane, imbecile, feebleminded, or epileptic. Man may not marry mother, daughter, grandmother, granddaughter, sister, half sister, aunt, niece, first cousin. Statute prohibits marriage between grandparents and grandchildren of every degree.

MONTANA

License issued by clerk of district court of county in which marriage is to take place. Cost of license, $2.25. Minimum ages: male, 18; female, 16. Parental consent necessary when male is under 21, female under 18. Blood test required. No marriage between whites and blacks or yellows. No marriage of the feeble-minded. Man may not marry mother, daughter, grandmother, granddaughter, sister, half sister, aunt, niece, first cousin. Statute prohibits marriage between ancestors and descendants.

NEBRASKA

License issued by county judge of county where marriage is to take place. Cost of license, $2.00. Minimum ages: male, 18; female, 16. Parental consent necessary when under 21. Blood test required. Two witnesses required. No marriage between whites and blacks or yellows. Idiots may not marry. Man may not marry mother, daughter, grandmother, granddaughter, sister, aunt, niece, first cousin.

NEVADA

License issued by clerk of any county in the state. Cost of license, $5.00. Minimum ages: male,

18; female, 16. Parental consent necessary when male is under 21, female under 18. No blood test required. Ministerial license necessary. Two witnesses required. No marriage of white with black, yellow, or red. No marriage of venereals, insane, or idiots. Man may not marry mother, daughter, grandmother, granddaughter, sister, aunt, niece, grandaunt, great-grandaunt, first cousin, first cousin once removed, or anyone of closer kin than second cousin.

NEW HAMPSHIRE

Certificate of intention must be filed with clerk of town in which either party resides; if nonresidents, with clerk of county in which marriage is to be solemnized. Cost of license, $3.00. Waiting period of license, 5 days. Minimum ages: male, 14; female, 13. Parental consent necessary when male is under 20, female under 18. Blood test required. No racial distinctions. No marriage of epileptics, imbeciles, feeble-minded, idiots, or insane. Man may not marry daughter, granddaughter, sister, aunt, niece, first cousin, father's widow, son's widow, grandson's widow, mother-in-law, or stepdaughter.

NEW JERSEY

License issued in first-class cities by clerk of city, elsewhere by registrar of vital statistics; if there be no registrar, by clerk of the municipality or assessor of taxes or their deputies. Cost of license, $3.00.

Waiting period for license, 72 hours. It shall be issued in the municipality in which the woman lives; if she is nonresident, in the municipality in which the man lives; if both are nonresident, in the municipality in which the marriage is to take place. Minimum ages: male, 18; female, 16. Parental consent necessary when male is under 21, female under 18. Blood test required. Two witnesses necessary. No racial restrictions. No marriage of venereals, narcotics, imbeciles, epileptics, or insane. Man may not marry mother, daughter, grandmother, granddaughter, sister, half sister, niece, half niece, aunt, half aunt. Marriage between ancestors and descendants prohibited.

NEW MEXICO

License issued by county clerk of county in which marriage will take place. Cost of license, $5.00. Minimum ages: male, 18; female, 16. Parental consent necessary when male is under 21, female under 18. Blood test required. Two witnesses required. No racial restrictions. Man may not marry mother, daughter, grandmother, granddaughter, sister, half sister, aunt, niece. Marriage between grandparents and grandchildren of every degree prohibited. Cousins may marry.

NEW YORK

License issued by clerk of town or city in which woman resides; if she is nonresident, in town in which marriage will take place. Cost of license,

$2.00. Waiting period after license is issued, 24 hours. Minimum ages: male, 16; female, 14. Parental consent necessary when man is under 21, woman under 18. Blood test required. In New York City all clergymen must register with the city clerk before they are permitted to solemnize marriages. One witness in addition to officiant. No racial restrictions. No marriage of idiots, insane, or venereals. Man may not marry mother, daughter, grandmother, granddaughter, sister, half sister, aunt, niece. Marriages between ancestors and descendants prohibited.

NORTH CAROLINA

License issued by registrar of deeds of county in which marriage is to take place. Cost of license, $5.00. Minimum age: 16 for both sexes. Parental consent necessary when under 18. Blood test required. One or more witnesses. No marriage of whites with reds or blacks to the third generation. No marriage of venereals, idiots, or imbeciles. Insane person permitted to marry after eugenic sterilization. No marriage of those afflicted with tuberculosis in the infectious stages. Man may not marry mother, daughter, grandmother, granddaughter, sister, aunt, niece, first cousin, double first cousin.

NORTH DAKOTA

License issued by judge of county in which either party resides. If that county be unorganized, then by the county to which it is attached for judicial purposes. No marriage of nonresidents. Cost of license, $1.00. Minimum ages: male, 18; female, 15. Parental consent necessary when male is under 21, female under 18. Blood test required. No marriage of white with black. No marriage of drunkards, imbeciles, criminals, idiots, feeble-minded, or insane, except when woman is over forty-five. Man may not marry mother, daughter, grandmother, granddaughter, sister, half sister, aunt, niece, first cousin, half first cousin. Marriage between grandparents and grandchildren of every degree prohibited.

OHIO

License issued by probate judge of county in which woman resides. Cost of license, $2.15. Waiting period for license, 5 days. No marriage of nonresidents. Minimum ages: male, 18; female, 16. Parental consent necessary when under 21. Blood test required. Minister must obtain a license from probate judge of the county before he can officiate at ceremony. No racial restrictions. No marriage of habitual drunkards, epileptics, narcotics, imbeciles, or insane. Man may not marry mother, daughter, grandmother, granddaughter, sister, aunt, niece, grandaunt, great-grandaunt, first cousin, grandniece, great-grandniece, first cousin once removed.

OKLAHOMA

License issued by judge or clerk of county court of county in which marriage is to be solemnized. Cost of license, $3.00. Minimum ages: male, 18; female, 15. Parental consent necessary when male is under 21, female under 18. Blood test required. Minister must file his credentials with judge of the county. Two witnesses necessary. No marriage of blacks with other races. Man may not marry mother, daughter, grandmother, granddaughter, sister, half sister, aunt, niece, first cousin, second cousin, stepmother, stepdaughter. Marriage between ancestors and descendants of any degree prohibited.

OREGON

License issued by clerk or any county. Cost of license, $3.00. Waiting period for license, 3 days. Minimum ages: male, 18; female, 15. Parental consent necessary when male is under 21, female under 18. Blood test required. Clergyman must file credentials with county clerk. Two witnesses required. No marriage of white with either black or yellow having one-fourth such blood. Man may not marry mother, daughter, granddaughter, sister, half sister, aunt, half aunt, niece, half niece, first cousin, half first cousin.

PENNSYLVANIA

License issued by clerk of orphans' court of county in which either resides or in which marriage is to be solemnized. Cost of license, $3.00. Waiting period for license, 3 days. Minimum ages: 16 for both sexes. Parental consent necessary when under 21. Blood test required. No marriage for imbeciles, epileptics, persons of unsound mind, or persons under the influence of intoxicating liquors or narcotics. No marriage for those afflicted with a transmissible disease. Man may not marry mother, daughter, grandmother, granddaughter, sister, aunt, niece, first cousin, stepmother, stepdaughter, daughter-in-law, wife's granddaughter.

RHODE ISLAND

License issued by clerk of town or city in which either resides; if nonresidents, town or city in which ceremony will be performed. Cost of license, $2.00. Waiting period for license, 5 days. Minimum ages: male, 18; female, 16. Parental consent necessary when under 21. Blood test required. Clergyman must secure license from clerk of town or city. Two witnesses required at ceremony. No racial restrictions. No marriage of lunatics. Man may not marry mother, daughter, grandmother, granddaughter, sister, aunt, niece, stepmother, daughter-in-law, grandfather's wife, grandson's wife, mother-in-law, stepdaughter, wife's grandmother, wife's granddaughter.

SOUTH CAROLINA

License issued by judge of probate court. Cost of license, $2.00. Waiting period for license, 24 hours. Minimum ages: male, 14; female, 12. Parental consent necessary when either party is under 18. No blood test required. Whites may not marry blacks, mulattoes, or reds. Idiots and lunatics may not marry. Man may not marry mother, daughter, grandmother, granddaughter, sister, aunt, niece, stepmother, son's wife, grandfather's wife, grandson's wife, wife's mother, stepdaughter, wife's grandmother, wife's granddaughter.

SOUTH DAKOTA

License issued by clerk of court of county in which marriage is to be solemnized. Cost of license, $2.50. Minimum ages: male, 18; female, 15. Parental consent necessary when male is under 21, female under 18. Blood test required. Two witnesses necessary. Whites may not marry blacks, browns, or yellows. Man may not marry mother, daughter, grandmother, granddaughter, sister, half sister, aunt, niece, first cousin, half first cousin, son's wife. No marriage between ancestors and descendants.

TENNESSEE

License issued by clerk of county court of county where female resides or where marriage is to be solemnized. Cost of license, $2.00. Waiting period for license, 3 days. Minimum ages: 16 for both sexes. Written parental consent necessary when under 21. Blood test required. Whites may not marry blacks to the third generation. Those of unsound mind may not marry. Man may not marry mother, daughter, grandmother, granddaughter, sister, half sister, aunt, niece, half niece, grandniece, half grandniece, great-grandniece, stepmother, son's wife, grandson's wife, stepdaughter, wife's granddaughter, any lineal descendant of a spouse, spouse of any lineal descendant.

TEXAS

License issued by clerk of any county. Cost of license, $3.00. Minimum ages: male, 16; female, 14. Written parental consent necessary when male is under 21, female under 18. Blood test required. No marriage between whites and blacks. Man may not marry mother, daughter, granddaughter, sister, half sister, aunt, half aunt, niece, half niece, father's widow, son's widow, stepdaughter, wife's granddaughter.

UTAH

License issued by clerk of county in which woman resides unless she be eighteen years or older, or a widow, in which case it may be issued in any county upon written application. Cost of license, $2.50. Minimum ages: male, 16; female, 14. Parental consent necessary when male is under 21, female under 18. Blood test required. Two witnesses necessary. Whites may not marry blacks or yellows. Man may not marry mother, daughter, grandmother, granddaughter, sister, half sister, aunt, niece, grandaunt, first cousin, grandniece, first cousin once removed.

VERMONT

Certificate authorizing marriage issued by clerk of town where man resides; if he is nonresident, by clerk of town where woman resides; if both are nonresident, by clerk of town where marriage will be solemnized. Cost of license, $3.00. Waiting period after license is issued, 5 days. Minimum ages: male, 18; female, 16. Parental consent necessary when male is under 21, female under 18. Blood test required. No racial restrictions. No marriage of those *non compos mentis*. Man may not marry mother, daughter, grandmother, granddaughter, sister, aunt, niece, stepmother, son's wife, grandfather's wife, grandson's wife, wife's mother, stepdaughter, wife's grandmother, wife's granddaughter. The restriction in these latter cases stands whether the marriage is dissolved by death or by divorce.

VIRGINIA

License issued by clerk of circuit court of county in which female resides; in case she is nonresident, county in which marriage is to be solemnized. Cost of license, $4.00. Minimum ages: male, 18; female, 16. Parental consent necessary when under 21. Blood test required. Surety bond of $500 required of clergymen before authorization by circuit court to perform ceremony. Whites may marry whites only. No marriage of habitual criminals, idiots, imbeciles, epileptics, insane, or venereals. Man may not marry mother, daughter, grandmother, granddaughter, sister, half sister, aunt, niece, stepmother, son's wife, wife's daughter, wife's granddaughter. Prohibition stands in most instances whether the relationship is dissolved by death or divorce.

WASHINGTON

License issued by county auditor. Cost of license, $5.00. Waiting period for license, 3 days. Minimum ages: no statutory age minimum for males; female, 15. Parental consent necessary when male is under 21, female under 18. No blood test required. Two witnesses necessary. No racial restrictions. No marriage for drunkards, habitual criminals, epileptics, imbeciles, feeble-minded, idiots, insane, venereals, or those afflicted with tuberculosis in an advanced degree, except when woman is forty-five or over. Man may not marry mother, daughter, grandmother, granddaughter, sister, aunt, half aunt, niece, half niece, grandaunt, great-grandaunt, first cousin, half first cousin, grandniece, great-grandniece, first cousin once removed, half first cousin once removed.

WEST VIRGINIA

License issued by clerk or county court of county in which female usually resides. Cost of license, $2.00. Waiting period for license, 3 days. Minimum ages: male, 18; female, 16. Parental consent necessary when under 21. Blood test required. Minister's credentials to perform marriage issued by either circuit or county court. Surety bond of $1,500 required. No marriages between whites and blacks. Man may not marry mother, daughter, grandmother, granddaughter, sister, half sister, aunt, niece, wife of nephew, first cousin, double first cousin, stepmother, son's wife, wife's daughter, wife's grandmother, wife's granddaughter. Prohibition stands in most cases whether the relationship has been dissolved by divorce or by death.

WISCONSIN

License issued by clerk of county in which either party resides; if nonresidents, county in which marriage will be solemnized. Cost of license, $1.00. Waiting period for license, 5 days. Minimum ages: male, 18; female, 15. Parental consent necessary when male is under 21, female under 18. Blood test required. Ministers must receive certificate from clerk of circuit court before they are authorized to perform marriage ceremony. Two witnesses required. No racial restrictions. No marriage of idiots, insane, epileptics, or feeble-minded. Man may not marry mother, daughter, grandmother, granddaughter, sister, aunt, niece, grandaunt, great-grandaunt, first cousin except when female is over fifty years of age, grandniece, great-grandniece, first cousin once removed. Marriage of persons nearer of kin than second cousins is prohibited except that first cousins may marry when the woman is over fifty years of age.

WYOMING

License issued by clerk of county in which marriage is to take place. Cost of license, $2.00. Minimum ages: male, 18; female, 16. Parental consent necessary when under 21. Blood test required. Two witnesses required. White may not marry black, mulatto, or yellow. Man may not marry mother, daughter, grandmother, granddaughter, sister, half sister, aunt, niece.

THE TERRITORIES

CANAL ZONE

Cost of license, $2.00. Minimum age: male, 17; female, 14. Parental consent necessary when male is under 21, female under 18. No blood test required.

GUAM

Cost of license, $2.50. Minimum ages: male, 18; female, 16. Parental consent necessary when male is under 21, female under 18. No blood test required.

PUERTO RICO

Cost of license, no charge. Minimum ages: male, 18; female, 16. Parental consent necessary when under 21. No blood test, but a medical certificate is required.

VIRGIN ISLANDS

Cost of license, 40¢. Waiting period for license, 8 days. Minimum ages: male, 16; female, 14. Parental consent necessary when male is under 21, female under 18. No blood test required.

STATE LAWS ON DIVORCE

ALABAMA

Grounds for divorce are: adultery, cruelty, desertion, nonsupport, alcoholism, felony, impotency, pregnancy at marriage, drug addiction, violence, crime against nature, 5 years' insanity. Residence time, 1 year; exceptions are to be noted. Time between interlocutory and final decrees, none. Sixty days to remarry.

ARIZONA

Grounds for divorce are: adultery, cruelty, desertion, nonsupport, alcoholism, felony, impotency, pregnancy at marriage, indignities, separation no cohabitation—5 years. Residence time, 1 year. Time between interlocutory and final decrees, none. One year to remarry.

ARKANSAS

Grounds for divorce are: adultery, cruelty, desertion, alcoholism, felony, impotency, indignities, separation no cohabitation—3 years, 3 years' insanity. Residence time, 3 months. Time between interlocutory and final decrees, none.

CALIFORNIA

Grounds for divorce are: adultery, cruelty, desertion, nonsupport, alcoholism, felony, 5 years' insanity. Residence time, 1 year. Time between interlocutory and final decrees, 1 year.

COLORADO

Grounds for divorce are: adultery, cruelty, desertion, nonsupport, alcoholism, felony, impotency, drug addiction, 5 years' insanity. Residence time, 1 year. Time between interlocutory and final decrees, none.

CONNECTICUT

Grounds for divorce are: adultery, cruelty, desertion, alcoholism, felony, fraudulent contract, 5 years' insanity. Residence time, 3 years. Time between interlocutory and final decrees, none.

DELAWARE

Grounds for divorce are: adultery, cruelty, desertion, nonsupport, alcoholism, felony, 5 years' insanity, separation no cohabitation—3 years. Residence time, 2 years; exceptions are to be noted. Time between interlocutory and final decrees, 3 months.

DISTRICT OF COLUMBIA

Grounds for divorce are: adultery, cruelty, desertion, felony, separation no cohabitation—5 years, separation for 2 years after decree for same. Residence time, 2 years; exceptions are to be noted. Time between interlocutory and final decrees, 6 months.

FLORIDA

Grounds for divorce are: adultery, cruelty, desertion, alcoholism, impotency, violence. Residence time, 6 months. Time between interlocutory and final decrees, none.

GEORGIA

Grounds for divorce are: adultery, cruelty, desertion, alcoholism, felony, impotency, pregnancy at marriage, fraudulent contract, 3 years insanity. Residence time, 6 months. Time between interlocutory and final decrees, determined by court order. Thirty days to remarry. Adultery cases, remarriage in discretion of court.

IDAHO

Grounds for divorce are: adultery, cruelty, desertion, nonsupport, alcoholism, felony, separation no cohabitation—5 years, 3 years insanity. Residence time, 6 weeks. Time between interlocutory and final decrees, none.

ILLINOIS

Requires 60 days' notice of intention to sue. Grounds for divorce are: adultery, cruelty, desertion, alcoholism, felony, impotency, violence, loathesome disease. Residence time, 1 year. Time between interlocutory and final decrees, none.

INDIANA

Grounds for divorce are: adultery, cruelty, desertion, nonsupport, alcoholism, felony, impotency, 5 years insanity. Residence time, 1 year. Time between interlocutory and final decrees, none.

IOWA

Grounds for divorce are: adultery, cruelty, desertion, alcoholism, felony, pregnancy at marriage. Residence time, 1 year. Time between interlocutory and final decrees, none. One year to remarry.

KANSAS

Grounds for divorce are: adultery, cruelty, desertion, nonsupport, alcoholism, felony, impotency, pregnancy at marriage, fraudulent contract, 5 years insanity. Residence time, 1 year. Time between interlocutory and final decrees, none. Six months to remarry.

KENTUCKY

Grounds for divorce are: adultery, cruelty, desertion, alcoholism, felony, impotency, pregnancy at marriage, fraudulent contract, loathesome disease, joining religious order disbelieving in marriage, unchaste behavior after marriage, separation no cohabitation—5 years, 5 years insanity. Residence time, 1 year. Time between interlocutory and final decrees, none.

LOUISIANA

Grounds for divorce are: adultery, cruelty, desertion, nonsupport, alcoholism, felony, no reconciliation for 1 year after judgment of separation, if guilty spouse is sentenced to infamous punishment, indignities, violence, separation for 2 years after decree for same. Residence time, 1 year; exceptions are to be noted. Time between interlocutory and final decrees, none.

MAINE

Grounds for divorce are: adultery, cruelty, desertion, nonsupport, alcoholism, impotency, drug addiction, violence. Residence time, 1 year. Time between interlocutory and final decrees, none.

MARYLAND

Grounds for divorce are: adultery, desertion, felony, impotency, unchastity of wife prior to marriage, separation no cohabitation—3 years, 3 years insanity. Residence time, 1 year; exceptions are to be noted. Time between interlocutory and final decrees, none.

MASSACHUSETTS

Grounds for divorce are: adultery, cruelty, desertion, nonsupport, alcoholism, felony, impotency, drug addiction. Residence time, 5 years; exceptions are to be noted. Time between interlocutory and final decrees, 6 months. Defendant must wait two years to remarry.

MICHIGAN

Grounds for divorce are: adultery, cruelty, desertion, nonsupport, alcoholism, felony, impotency. Residence time, 1 year. Time between interlocutory and final decrees, none.

MINNESOTA

Grounds for divorce are: adultery, cruelty, desertion, alcoholism, felony, impotency, separation no cohabitation—5 years, 5 years insanity, separation for 5 years after decree for same. Residence time, 1 year. Time between interlocutory and final decrees, none. Six months to remarry.

MISSISSIPPI

Grounds for divorce are: adultery, cruelty, desertion, alcoholism, felony, impotency, pregnancy at marriage, drug addiction. Residence time, 1 year. Time between interlocutory and final decrees, none. Adultery cases, remarriage in discretion of court.

MISSOURI

Grounds for divorce are: adultery, cruelty, desertion, nonsupport, alcoholism, felony, impotency, pregnancy at marriage, indignities, husband being a vagrant. Residence time, 1 year. Time between interlocutory and final decrees, none.

MONTANA

Grounds for divorce are: adultery, cruelty, desertion, nonsupport, alcoholism, felony, 5 years insanity. Residence time, 1 year. Time between interlocutory and final decrees, none.

NEBRASKA

Grounds for divorce are: adultery, cruelty, desertion, nonsupport, alcoholism, felony, impotency, 5 years insanity. Residence time, 2 years; exceptions are to be noted. Time between interlocutory and final decrees, 6 months.

NEVADA

Grounds for divorce are: adultery, cruelty, desertion, nonsupport, alcoholism, felony, impotency, separation no cohabitation—3 years, 2 years insanity. Residence time, 6 weeks. Time between interlocutory and final decrees, none.

NEW HAMPSHIRE

Grounds for divorce are: adultery, cruelty, desertion, nonsupport, alcoholism, felony, impotency, joining religious order disbelieving in marriage, separation no cohabitation—3 years. Residence time, 1 year; exceptions are to be noted. Time between interlocutory and final decrees, none.

NEW JERSEY

Grounds for divorce are: adultery, cruelty, desertion. Residence time, 2 years. Time between interlocutory and final decrees, 3 months.

NEW MEXICO

Grounds for divorce are: adultery, cruelty, desertion, nonsupport, alcoholism, felony, impotency, pregnancy at marriage, 5 years insanity. Residence time, 1 year; exceptions are to be noted. Time between interlocutory and final decrees, none.

NEW YORK

Only ground for divorce is adultery. Residence time, 1 year; exceptions are to be noted. Time between interlocutory and final decrees, 3 months. Plaintiff may remarry in 3 months; defendant may not remarry before three years without consent of court; exceptions are to be noted.

NORTH CAROLINA

Grounds for divorce are: adultery, impotency, pregnancy at marriage, crime against nature, 10 years insanity. Residence time, 6 months. Time between interlocutory and final decrees, none.

NORTH DAKOTA

Grounds for divorce are: adultery, cruelty, desertion, nonsupport, alcoholism, felony, 5 years insanity. Residence time, 1 year. Time between interlocutory and final decrees, determined by court order. Adultery cases, remarriage in discretion of court.

OHIO

Grounds for divorce are: adultery, cruelty, desertion, nonsupport, alcoholism, felony, impotency, fraudulent contract. Residence time, 1 year. Time between interlocutory and final decress, none.

OKLAHOMA

Grounds for divorce are: adultery, cruelty, desertion, nonsupport, alcoholism, felony, impotency, pregnancy at marriage, fraudulent contract, 5 years insanity. Residence time, 1 year. Time between interlocutory and final decrees, 6 months.

OREGON

Grounds for divorce are: adultery, cruelty, desertion, alcoholism, felony, impotency, indignities, 5 years insanity. Residence time, 1 year. Time between interlocutory and final decrees, none. Six months to remarry.

PENNSYLVANIA

Grounds for divorce are: adultery, cruelty, desertion, felony, impotency, fraudulent contract, indignities. Residence time, 1 year. Time between interlocutory and final decrees, none.

RHODE ISLAND

Grounds for divorce are: adultery, cruelty, desertion, nonsupport, alcoholism, felony, impotency, drug addiction, any gross misbehavior or wickedness, 5 years insanity, separation no cohabitation— 10 years. Residence time, 2 years. Time between interlocutory and final decrees, 6 months.

SOUTH CAROLINA

Grounds for divorce: adultery, cruelty, desertion, alcoholism. Residence time, 1 year. Time between interlocutory and final decrees, none.

SOUTH DAKOTA

Grounds for divorce: adultery, cruelty, desertion, nonsupport, alcoholism, felony, 5 years insanity. Residence time, 1 year; exceptions are to be noted. Time between interlocutory and final decrees, none.

TENNESSEE

Grounds for divorce are: adultery, desertion, alcoholism, felony, impotency, violence, indignities. Residence time, 1 year. Time between interlocutory and final decrees, none.

TEXAS

Grounds for divorce are: adultery, cruelty, desertion, felony, 5 years insanity, separation no cohabitation—10 years. Residence time, 1 year. Time between interlocutory and final decrees, none. Except in cruelty cases, one year to remarry.

UTAH

Grounds for divorce are: adultery, cruelty, desertion, nonsupport, alcoholism, felony, impotency, separation for 3 years after decree for same, 5 years insanity. Residence time, 3 months. Time between interlocutory and final decrees, 3 months.

VERMONT

Grounds for divorce are: adultery, cruelty, desertion, nonsupport, felony, separation no cohabitation—3 years, 5 years insanity. Residence time, 1 year; exceptions are to be noted. Time between interlocutory and final decrees, 6 months. Plaintiff, six months; defendant, two years, to remarry.

VIRGINIA

Grounds for divorce are: adultery, desertion, felony, impotency, pregnancy at marriage, wife being a prostitute, indignities. Residence time, 1 year. Time between interlocutory and final decrees, none. Four months to remarry; exceptions are to be noted.

WASHINGTON

Grounds for divorce are: adultery, cruelty, desertion, nonsupport, alcoholism, felony, impotency, fraudulent contract, indignities, separation no cohabitation—5 years, 2 years insanity. Residence time, 1 year. Time between interlocutory and final decrees, none.

WEST VIRGINIA

Grounds for divorce are: adultery, cruelty, desertion, alcoholism, felony, drug addiction. No minimum residence required in adultery cases; otherwise, residence time, 2 years; exceptions are to be noted. Time between interlocutory and final decrees, none. Sixty days to remarry. Adultery cases, remarriage in discretion of court.

WISCONSIN

Grounds for divorce are: adultery, cruelty, desertion, nonsupport, alcoholism, felony, impotency, separation no cohabitation—5 years, separation for 5 years after decree for same. Residence time, 1 year; exceptions are to be noted. Time between interlocutory and final decrees, 1 year.

WYOMING

Grounds for divorce are: adultery, cruelty, desertion, nonsupport, alcoholism, felony, impotency, pregnancy at marriage, indignities, husband being a vagrant, 2 years insanity. Residence time, 60 days. Time between interlocutory and final decrees, none.

Annulment of Marriage

Annulment is quite a different thing from divorce. When a fraud of some kind has been practiced in a marriage, the court may rule that the marriage has never been legalized and set it aside. Insanity, impotency, conviction of felony, prior marriage having never been dissolved, failure to complete conditions promised which may involve property or physical relationships—any or all of these may be the basis for annulment. While the Roman Catholic Church will not recognize divorce, it does dissolve many marriages because of inability or lack of desire to complete the contract.

INDEX